Praise for Raimond Gaita

ROMULUS, MY FATHER

'Extraordinary and beautiful...a profound meditation on love and death, madness and truth, judgment and compassion.'
RICHARD FLANAGAN, SUNDAY AGE

'The moving intensity of the narrative makes *Romulus, My Father* a triumph.'
FRANKFURT ALLGEMEINE ZEITUNG

'consistently astounding...a memoir of absolutely compelling tragi-comic quality.'
PETER CRAVEN, AUSTRALIAN

'A marvellous book...an original meditation on life itself: character, conversation, friendship, morality and the terror of insanity.'
SPECTATOR

'A gift to a man, to his vision of life...a story marked by constant wonder and the acceptance of life.'
LA REALIDAD

'A rare and passionate book, the like of which has seldom been seen in Australia.'
SYDNEY MORNING HERALD

A COMMON HUMANITY: THINKING ABOUT LOVE & TRUTH & JUSTICE

'Philosophy at its most profound.'
JEAN CURTHOYS, AUSTRALIAN BOOK REVIEW

'On every page of Gaita's work—all his work—one hears a distinctive, unrelentingly serious and powerful voice.

In *Romulus* its tone is lyrical and affecting, in *Good and Evil* philosophical and exacting... *A Common Humanity* is a work of both the writer and philosopher. It is a rare and distinguished contribution to our public life.'
MARTIN KRYGIER, AUSTRALIAN'S REVIEW OF BOOKS

'As eloquent as it is affecting.'
ECONOMIST, BOOKS OF THE YEAR, 2000

'Profound and original'
TIMES LITERARY SUPPLEMENT

'A wise and beautifully written book...a wonderful example of how philosophy can still speak without any condescension.'
SIMON CRITCHLEY

GOOD AND EVIL:
AN ABSOLUTE CONCEPTION

'I would not have believed that a work in moral philosophy could, in our present age, have such depth, brilliance and force.'
NORMAN MALCOLM

'Outstanding.'
ALASDAIR MACINTYRE

'A superb, richly textured discussion which engages directly with real people and their deeply serious moral concerns.'
TIMES HIGHER EDUCATION SUPPLEMENT

'Genuinely moving...A wonderful book.'
STANLEY HAUERWAS

'Profound...splendidly original and insightful discussions.'
R. A. DUFF, PHILOSOPHICAL BOOKS

'A Socratic attempt to call moral philosophy back to seriousness...one of the deepest works on ethics I have read.'
LARS HERTZBERG, PHILOSOPHICAL INVESTIGATIONS

RAIMOND GAITA

The philosopher's dog

Routledge
Taylor & Francis Group

LONDON AND NEW YORK

First published in 2002
by The Text Publishing Company, Australia

This edition first published 2003
by Routledge
11 New Fetter Lane, London EC4P 4EE

Routledge is an imprint of the Taylor & Francis Group

© 2002, 2003 Raimond Gaita

Typeset in 13/18.4 Centaur MT by
Lynne Hamilton
Printed and bound in Great Britain by
MPG Books Ltd, Bodmin

British Library Cataloguing in Publication Data
A catalogue record for this book is available
from the British Library

Library of Congress Cataloging in Publication Data
A catalog record for this book has been requested

ISBN 0 415 30907 7 hbk

Photograph of the author with Gypsy on page vi by Konrad Winkler

For Cora Diamond

'The difference between human beings and animals is not to be discovered by studies of Washoe or the activities of dolphins. It is not that sort of study or ethology or evolutionary theory that is going to tell us the difference between us and animals: the difference is, as I have suggested, a central concept for human life and is more an object of contemplation than observation (though that might be misunderstood; I am not suggesting it is a matter of intuition). One source of confusion here is that we fail to distinguish between 'the difference between animals and people' and 'the differences between animals and people'; the same sort of confusion occurs in discussions of the relationship of men and women. In both cases people appeal to scientific evidence to show that 'the difference' is not as deep as we think; but all that such evidence can show, or show directly, is that the differences are less sharp than we think. In the case of the difference between animals and people, it is clear that we form the idea of this difference, create the concept of the difference, knowing perfectly well the overwhelmingly obvious similarities.'   *Cora Diamond*

'God went forth to create the world, and he took his dog with him.'
Kato Indian creation story

Contents

Introduction

Thirty years ago I thought I would write a book about nature, inspired mostly by my experiences in the mountains. I would have included a small section about animals. Now I've written a book that has a chapter on mountains and is mostly about animals, though butterflies, spiders and bees get a relatively long chapter of their own. Human beings appear throughout. This book is about our creatureliness.

The book I intended to write thirty years ago would have been a straightforwardly academic book about human beings in their relation to nature. When I wrote *Romulus, My Father* I discovered that I liked telling stories about animals. *The Philosopher's Dog* is a mixture of story-telling and philosophical reflection on the stories I tell. It's personal, not because there are personal revelations in it nor, I hope, because it's self absorbed, but because I write almost exclusively about the animals I've known. For the most part I write about them in the context of family life with my father and his friend

Pantelimon Hora and my wife and my children. People sometimes ask me what the relation is between philosophy and my life. *The Philosopher's Dog* provides part of an answer.

Some readers will be surprised that there are no references in this book to extensive empirical studies of the capacities of animals, especially of clever wild animals like dolphins and apes. The absence of such references is not an oversight. The personal form of the book expresses one part of its mildly didactic purpose, which is to show how much one can learn about our relations to animals (including our moral relations to them) by reflection of a philosophical kind on our lives with ordinary domestic pets—birds, dogs and cats.

Philosophy and story-telling require, in my experience, different casts of mind. Generally philosophy aims straight and abstractly for the point, rushing past the kind of details that bring a story to life. Some of the philosophy in *The Philosopher's Dog* is difficult. All of it is philosophising on the job, so to speak. None of it is philosophy made popular. To bring philosophy and story-telling together, without turning the stories into long-winded philosophical examples and without compromising the philosophy for the sake of a good story, was for me by far the hardest challenge in writing this book. It is for readers to judge whether I have risen to it. My advice to the reader who finds some of the philosophical sections difficult is to read on, though slowly, and to return to the difficult sections when she has finished the book, remembering that all philosophy benefits from, and most philosophy requires, more than one reading.

My father's attitude to animals affected me profoundly. I could not write about my relation to animals without telling again some of the stories that I told in *Romulus, My Father*, though they are told differently and set in a different context. I hope that the readers of *Romulus* will not mind reading again and more about Jack the cockatoo and Orlaf the dog.

Michael Heyward suggested that I write this book. Were it not for his faith in it I would have long ago abandoned it. In *Romulus, My Father* I tell how my father had the capacity to eye a piece of steel, scrape a line on it with his thumb, and to cut it to within a millimetre of accuracy. When Michael looks at a page of my work, he seems to have a comparable gift.

Tony Bruce, my publisher at Routledge also encouraged me to write this book, pretty much from when I began to think about it. For that I am grateful. I am even more grateful that he has enthusiastically stuck by this quite unclassifiable book.

Friends and Companions

The white patch in a dark blue sky changed shape as he turned or rose or descended. Often in winter the grass was also white, thick with frost until ten and even eleven in the morning. In summer it grew high and yellow and was especially beautiful in the late afternoon if the wind joined with the sun to transform entire paddocks into waves of moving grass, golden and tipped with silver. The thrill of seeing him in that landscape, against that sky, imprinted an image on my mind that is as vivid now as the sight of him was more than forty years ago. He was Jack, our cockatoo, and he was following me to school, flying a bit, then sitting on the handlebars of my bike before flying some more.

Jack was much more my father's pet than mine. In fact, I'm not sure that I should say he was mine at all. We lived together on terms he dictated, indifferent to my need to possess him, giving or withholding affection as he pleased. Nonetheless, he was a great joy to me and never more so than when he followed me to school. When he sat on my handlebars I felt we were friends. I even dared hope that we were comrades. But back at home, in the evening of the same day that he followed me to school, if I moved to stroke his crest he was as likely as not to bite me just because he felt like it.

He was fiercely loyal to one person at a time and that person was my father except once when my father was in hospital and his friend Pantelimon Hora looked after me at Frogmore, our chicken farm near Baringhup in central Victoria. During those months Jack transferred his loyalty to Hora rather than to me even though I had lived with him for years. 'Hey liew liew,' Hora used to say to Jack, sometimes to greet him and sometimes as though to ask, 'And how are things now?' The affection both men felt for Jack—the interest they took in him and his ways and the intimate knowledge of him that they shared—deepened, and was in turn deepened by, their friendship. More than thirty years after they had last seen Jack they greeted one another in the same way. 'Hey liew liew,' one would say. 'Hey liew liew,' the other would respond.

Hora delighted in Jack and often observed him with affectionate attention, sometimes chuckling at Jack's comical ways, at other times marvelling at his ingenuity. Jack soon made himself at home in the part of the house Hora occupied when he was with us, though he was never physically as intimate with Hora as he was with my father, never so ready to surrender himself to his petting. Nor, I suspect, did he ever entirely trust Hora to give him food of the quality that he fancied he deserved. Whenever Hora cooked spaghetti (which was almost every other evening) Jack waited patiently until it was ready and then made it known that he would like some. Always Hora gave him some on a separate plate. Always Jack tried what had been given him and then asked for some from Hora's plate. Only when he was satisfied that Hora's spaghetti was no better than his did he return to his plate.

As well as spaghetti Jack was especially fond of bread dipped in tea or coffee. Whenever we had a cup of either Jack would come down the side of his door to the level of the table to ask for his soaked bread. He ate many things that we did. Whenever it was something he had not eaten before he would nibble it ever so delicately, cock his head to see what to make of it, try it again and, after doing this a few times, he would usually eat it. Convinced that it would not harm him he relaxed, enjoying the excitement of something new and yielding to the pleasure of it. In this and many other small ways Jack came to share our world.

My father was in hospital for almost three months. When he came home Jack could not contain himself. He screeched, raised his crest, and allowed my father to stroke him on every part of his body, turning first on this side then on the other and then upside down, and all this for hours. For a day or two afterwards, when Hora tried to pet him, he raised his crest aggressively and even bit him once or twice. Jack simplified his emotions, overcoming without difficulty whatever conflicts he may have felt when confronted by two claimants for his loyalty. I, who loved both men dearly, fell prey for a short time to the pains of ambivalent attachment.

We are seldom physically as tender with birds as we are with cats and dogs, even when we have complex moral relations with birds— as we do with birds of prey, for example, whom we have trained, if not tamed. Accustomed to seeing birds in cages, our physical contact with them is often limited. We sometimes stroke them when they perch on our arms or shoulders, but we don't cuddle them. They stand stiffly on their legs, their bodies are not flexible, their contours don't fit ours. So it can seem, but it's not quite true.

Jack flew free and had the run of the house. He slept on the kitchen door on which he made himself at home by eating parts of it and the adjacent wall. Almost every morning he would climb down from his door and come into the bedroom in which my father and I were sleeping. The sound of his beak and claws alternately scraping on the kitchen door as he climbed down, and of him trying to open the bedroom door by pushing it with his head and retreating as it closed on him, usually woke us. But if my father remained asleep, or if he pretended to be asleep, Jack would perch on the bedstead until he opened his eyes. He would then jump under the blankets, poking his head out occasionally to kiss my father.

How does a cockatoo kiss? Like this. He puts the upper part of his beak onto your lips and, nibbling gently, runs it down to your lower lip, all the while saying 'tsk tsk tsk'. That, at any rate, is how Jack did it to my father, with unmistakable tenderness. My father would stroke him, under his wings, under his beak and on his chest and stomach. Sometimes he would cup his hands around Jack's head and return his kisses. The same sound—tsk, tsk, tsk—came from under the blankets together with an occasional squawk, sometimes of pleasure and sometimes of sudden but slight pain as my father inadvertently hurt him. Never, however, did I hear a squawk of fear or even anxiety, never anything that suggested Jack's trust of my father was qualified in the slightest degree.

My father worked in a blacksmith shop on a neighbouring farm some half a kilometre from our house. Jack often went with him.

Sometimes he would keep him company in the workshop, digging his beak into small heaps of screws or scraps of iron, placing some to one side, some to the other, as though he were sorting them. When he tired of this, he flew around the area looking to see what mischief he could do. He never had trouble finding it, but when he bit off all the bright plastic baubles on our neighbour's television antenna, my father was forced to cut his wing, compelled by the threat that Jack would otherwise be shot. Undeterred, Jack walked from our house to the blacksmith shop. Even with his wing cut he could fly a little, only in circles, but with practice he gained sufficient height to reach the antenna. So, for a time, to keep him out of trouble, my father tied a chain to his leg and weighted it down with an old sandal. If Jack tried hard enough he could drag the chain with its weight along the ground, but he must have reckoned that what he gained by doing this wasn't worth the trouble. Mostly he moved only within the five- or six-metre radius the chain allowed him without effort.

My father and I talked quite a bit to Jack. Generally, we asked him questions. 'So you're back, are you?' 'Would you like to come with us to fetch the cow?' 'Why don't you leave the dog in peace?' 'Why must you chew holes in the doors?' As a consequence he often had a quizzical air, but perhaps I imagined it. There was no doubt, however, that Jack was a highly intelligent bird. Occasionally we would catch him trying to whistle a tune he had heard on the wireless. He would whistle a little of it, forget how to go on, and would then screech, raise his crest and dance around on the chicken-wire fence in frustration. When he calmed down, he would usually get a little further until he would again forget how to go on. He did this often, but would stop if he noticed us observing him. Only when he believed no one could see him did he practise whistling tunes he had heard. We seldom talked cocky talk to him, and he seldom talked it to us. He talked a lot, but mostly to himself.

Close though Jack was to us, it seemed the conditional closeness of a creature that spends only part of its time earthbound. The thrill of seeing him high in that dark blue sky above a vast and empty landscape was partly an expression of the mysterious place that birds have in our lives. On the one hand, high there in the sky, completely free in his flight, he seemed alien to us, a being of a quite different and enviable kind, one who graced our lives with the gratuitous gift of his friendship. On the other hand, he was my pet cockatoo, who slept on the kitchen door, climbed into my father's bed and was now following me to school, soon to sit again on my handlebars for a few minutes, inviting me yet again to yield to the illusion that he might become as close to me as he was to my father.

When we moved from Frogmore to Maryborough, a nearby town, my father left Jack behind. He could not allow him to roam free in town for he was recklessly destructive. Nor could he bear to cage him. The feathers in his wing had grown again, and the sandal and chain were never intended to be a permanent means of keeping him earthbound. Jack used occasionally to fly off for days, sometimes even weeks, with passing flocks of cockatoos and we hoped that he would do so when he realised that we would not come home. It broke my father's heart to do this and he was troubled with guilt as he thought about Jack waiting futilely for our return.

More than a month passed before my father went back to see what had happened to Jack. He feared that if Jack were still at the house, perched on his pole above the fence, then either he would relent and take him to Maryborough where he would cage him against his better judgment, or Jack would take heart from the visit, only to have to face again the despair of waiting for someone who would not come. Jack wasn't there. We never saw him again.

Before Jack, and more deeply than Jack, Orloff was my first animal friend. He was a black greyhound cross, taller and more solid than most greyhounds. We inherited him from the people who lived at Frogmore before us. If I ever knew how old he was I have now forgotten, but the strength in his muscular body, and the speed with which he ran after rabbits and almost always caught them, make it certain that he was still quite young. If he came across a fence while chasing rabbits, he would angle his body to the side so that he could pass between two strands of wire without noticeably slowing down.

My childhood was troubled. Early in it my mother left my father, repeatedly returned and left again. Though he loved me profoundly and though I never doubted it, my father was not a physically affectionate man, so I turned to Orloff for warmth and comfort. Probably I would have done so even if my father were different, for I suspect there are ways in which a dog can come closer than a man to satisfying a child's unfulfilled need of a woman's touch.

For a time during our life in the country my father worked night shift and I was alone at night in our dilapidated farmhouse. Kilometres from the nearest town and ten minutes' walk from the nearest homestead, it had no electric lighting and creaked ominously in the wind. To cope with my fear I took Orloff to bed with me, grateful for his reassuring presence, but disappointed that he showed no interest in the stories that I listened to on the wireless until I fell asleep.

Years later, in adulthood, I was delighted to discover that some Aborigines measure the cold of a night by the number of dogs they need for warmth. A very cold night might be a three- or even a four-dog night. Remembering my need of Orloff, I was astonished at the contempt shown to the Aborigines by the person who told me this. For the same reason the disdain expressed in the old saying that he who sleeps with dogs must expect fleas is foreign to me, as is the disgust that many people feel at the idea of a dog on the bed, let alone in it. People often say that it spoils dogs to allow them on the bed but it needn't. There are other ways of disciplining dogs, of requiring that they curb their desires rather than yield to them at first impulse. The idea that if you relax discipline in one region then you will erode it everywhere needs as much qualification, I believe, in its application to dogs as to human beings.

When I went to school, six kilometres away, Orloff often accompanied me part of the way and he would be there, the same distance from the house, when I returned. Mostly I rode to school on my bike, but occasionally a neighbouring farmer would drive me. As I walked from the junction of the road and the rough track to our house Orloff would bound up to greet me with such enthusiasm that he would knock me over. Lying there in the long grass with him standing over me, legs astride my chest, licking me and making affectionate noises and wagging his tail so furiously that his entire body swayed with it, I felt he was my closest and truest friend and I loved him.

Probably only a child can place such innocent trust in a dog's fidelity. But I did not trust Orloff because, as a child, I believed false things about him. I did not think he was a person and as far as I remember I did not attribute to him capacities he did not possess. Nor, of course, did I believe that he was a machine or a bundle of conditioned reflexes. I was a child alone, deeply pained by family events, frightened by worse things in prospect and sometimes by my surroundings. The depth of my need and Orloff's intelligent and faithful response to it generated an intensity in my relationship to him that could not be captured by the idea of mere companionship.

People who find close and needful companionship with animals, especially with dogs, sometimes say that dogs are better than human beings. The misanthropy that is often expressed in such remarks is always sad. When I said that, as a boy, I felt that Orloff was my truest friend, I did not mean to disparage my school friends. But they could not satisfy, as Orloff did, my deep need of physical comfort, protection and security. I do not recall attributing false powers to him, but I did trust that he would protect me if I were in danger. For some children, that trust is an important dimension in their relationship to their dog, and often it does both child and dog good. Such children need reasonably big dogs.

In the event it was I who proved faithless to Orloff. Fascinated by Tarzan's chimp, I wrote to the Melbourne zoo, asking if they could give or sell me one. To my surprise, and even more Hora's— he was looking after me at the time—the zoo responded quickly and politely. 'Dear Master Gaita,' the letter began, raising my hopes that my request had been granted. Regrettably, it went on to say, it was against the zoo's policy to give or sell children chimps or any other kind of monkey, but perhaps I would consider a cat or a dog or some kind of bird. Incredulous that anyone could think such ordinary animals could satisfy someone who had dreamed of a chimp, I threw the letter away, but even as I did it I felt guilty towards Orloff for my treacherous desires. Not, though, towards Jack who had been giving me and everyone else except my father a hard time. He had bitten me, had been harassing the cats, biting their ears whenever they were at their milk bowl, and had taken to landing on Orloff's back and biting his ear whenever he wanted him to move or sometimes just for the malicious pleasure of it. A monkey, I thought, would give him his comeuppance.

Orloff took to roaming the paddocks many kilometres from home. One day a farmer told my father that a dog had been molesting sheep in the area and that he suspected it was Orloff. Desperately we hoped it wasn't so, because we knew the consequences if it were, but in our hearts we thought it likely and a sense of foreboding darkened our lives. A month or so later, Orloff came home with a rifle wound in his side. The bullet had hit low in his stomach where his greyhound build was low and thin and passed right through. My father tended his wounds with his remedy for anything external or liable to infection: methylated spirits, lanolin and spider's web.

A few weeks later we found Orloff dead one morning some twenty metres from the house. He had been bleeding from the mouth because he had been fed meat spiked with glass. He lay on the far side of a fence that separated the house and its yard from the paddocks beyond. Though I call it a yard, we did nothing to it to justify the domestic connotations of that word. A pile, some ten metres in diameter, of bottles and rusted food tins lay on the far side, but that was the only feature that marked a difference between what was on one side of the fence and what was on the other. Yet so tenderly did my father lift Orloff over the fence that I needed no words from him to know that he did it so that Orloff would be buried where his home had been.

As my father dug the grave, placed Orloff in it and buried him, I remembered our friendship. I thought of how painful it must have been for him to get home, his insides ravaged by the sharp glass. The fence had proved an impossible obstacle. We cried for him. It was the first time I had seen my father cry and the only time we cried together. For weeks I felt as though the pain in my chest would make it explode.

Sometimes people who are simple and good have a natural affinity with animals. In my childhood I knew such a man, one who seemed to me wholly innocent, gentle and kind. His name was Vacek Vilkovikas. Like my father he had come to Australia in the early 1950s on an assisted passage which required him to work for two years in repayment. We met him in a migrant workers' camp in central Victoria where he had been sent, as my father had, to build a reservoir. Soon after the work was finished Vacek lost his mind and he went to live between two large granite boulders on the side of a small mountain some fifteen kilometres from where my father and I lived. To protect himself from the weather he covered the boulders with whatever he could find and there he lived, contented I believe, for some years. His primitive home looked over one of the most beautiful vistas in the area, immediately onto neighbouring hills and beyond to the blue Pyrenees. In summer, Vacek's side of the hill was covered with high golden grass. Interspersed between granite boulders, some of them six metres high, were large cactus plants, with flowers of rich yellow, worthy heralds of the magnificent bluish-purple fruit that was to follow them. Together, the ancient grey rounded boulders and the cacti—especially when their fruit had been gouged open by birds—made the area look prehistoric. Vacek lived in that landscape as though in friendship with it.

A frugal man, he had saved a reasonable amount of money with which he bought himself a large Sunbeam motorbike, shaft-driven and with tyres the size of those on a small car, and also a rifle with telescopic sights with which to hunt rabbits. The rest of his money he left in the bank in Maldon, two or three kilometres away, taking out small amounts occasionally to buy what little he needed. Near to the boulders where he slept he built a small tin shed (I don't know why he didn't sleep in it) and there he kept various concoctions that he had pickled, sometimes in his urine. Visibly insane, he talked to himself, though never with the aggressive guttural explosions that mark some forms of insanity. He spoke as gently to himself as he did to others, sometimes barely audibly, furrowing his brow when he asked himself a question or extending his arm, palm upwards, to express helplessness or resignation.

Vacek's innocence showed in everything he did. It showed in the gentle quality of his madness and in his relation to animals, in his unaffected ease with them that seemed, strange though it may sound, to express a sense of equality with them. From time to time he came to stay with my father and me for a week or more. On one such occasion he bought some sausages for his dinner. While he was preparing his meal he left the sausages on the table and went to do something in another part of the house. When he came back the sausages were gone. Orloff was the obvious suspect. Vacek called Orloff to question him. Had he taken his sausages? The question was unnecessary because Orloff's expression was unmistakably that of a guilty dog. Vacek then told Orloff how disappointed he was. He told him that he had not dreamed that he would so miserably betray his trust. He implored him never to do anything like it again. Later, when he told Hora of the episode, Vacek swore that Orloff had promised that he would not.

Many of the stories I tell in this book are of relationships in which human beings need animals for companionship and comfort. Because of the ways in which need can distort and poison relationships we tend to be suspicious of it. To attempt to rid ourselves of need in order to prevent those distortions or, more desperately, in pursuit of an ideal of self-sufficiency, would be disastrous, however, were we to succeed. The need we have—often unfathomable—of other human beings is partly what conditions and yields to us our sense of their preciousness. The same is true of our relations to animals. The destructiveness of need is the negative dimension of its power to generate the highest forms of our relationships with them.

One of the wisest men I have known told me that we all need someone who will cry for us when we are dead. Humbled acknowledgment of our need is our best protection against foolish condescension to both human beings and animals. Our acknowledgment of need can enable us to see things more truly. The person who has rid himself of the need of others, who longs and grieves for no one, is not someone who is positioned to see things most clearly. And the person who does not need animals is not, if he condescends to those who do, better placed to understand the real possibilities in relations between human beings and animals. My father, a man who longed for company and who took exuberant pleasure in mingling with crowds, found, in his lonely life in our derelict farmhouse, companionship with Jack the cockatoo. Out of that need there developed a relationship the like of which I have never seen between a man and a bird. My own deep companionship with Orloff, my childhood sense of him as my truest friend, was in part a function of my need.

Animals can respond to our needs with surprising tenderness. Zac was the dog of my daughters Katie and Eva and of their mother Margaret. Like Orloff, he was, I think, none too bright, but also like Orloff he was good. He was in fact the best dog I have known. Just as cleverness is an overrated virtue in human beings, so cleverness is not the most important quality in dogs.

A black kelpie-labrador cross, Zac was, as Katie and Eva declared when they first set eyes on him, ex-zac-tly what they wanted. Sooner than expected he turned out also to be exactly what they—especially Eva—needed. Sitting on the back steps of her house, Eva confided her woes to him during a difficult and unrelievedly miserable period at school. As soon as he noticed she was distressed, he would climb onto her lap, put his paws over her shoulders and lick away her tears. Cynics will say he was after the salt in her tears, but it wasn't so. He didn't clamber onto her lap in response to her distress hoping she would cry. Nor did he change his demeanour when the tears came. The way he licked away her tears was of a piece with his own evident distress at her distress, and of a piece with the tenderness of his gestures, with the way he put his paws on her shoulders, and with the soft noises he made.

If ever a voice was raised in the house (not necessarily in anger) Zac would stand between the parties with a demeanour that was partly protective of the one he thought was under attack, or being reprimanded, and partly admonishing of the one he believed to be the aggressor. Being only imperfectly conversant with human ways, he could not always tell the difference between anger and, say, excitement, and comical situations would sometimes occur as he rushed to put himself between people. His intelligence was sometimes in doubt, but never his good heart.

When he was young the strength in Zac's bounds could take one's breath away. In his later years he declined rapidly when heart trouble set in. His pitiable appearance when he walked was compounded by a limp caused by a collapsed paw. His deterioration reminded me of my father's decline, which was also due to a heart condition. Both had been so strong when young. 'Can you believe what has become of me?' my father said, looking at his hands, which could no longer even hold tools. Zac didn't say this nor could he think it. Nonetheless the pathos of his condition was part of his story, a story that linked together his younger years and the years of his decline.

With the aid of medication Zac lived just long enough for Eva to finish her final exams at school. As she worked, he lay in her room and slept sometimes on her bed. He gave comfort to her at the beginning of her school days and at their end. Margaret and the girls scattered his ashes in the nearby schoolyard where they had often taken him for walks.

Between human beings friendship is constituted by standards that distinguish it from its false semblances and also from companionship. Friendship, Aristotle claimed, cannot exist between adults and children because it can truly exist only between equals and between those who have the wisdom and the will to rise to its demands. He would have scorned the idea that it could exist between human beings and animals.

The contrast between the reality of an emotion or a virtue and its counterfeit forms is fundamental to the characterisation of human life. Where would we be without love, devotion, loyalty, bravery and friendship, for example? A human being who was incapable of reflecting, perhaps because of severe brain damage, upon the distinctions between real love and infatuation, or between real loyalty and servility, would be incapable of love or loyalty, or any of the virtues that make for character or any of the emotions that make for a rich inner life. Is it therefore just anthropomorphism to attribute these feelings and virtues to animals?

I have written as though it is not, though I do not believe that the animals I have written about had reflective capacities. Slowly, and to some degree circuitously, I will try to explain why.

For a Dog?

A week before Gypsy's accident, an old woman was killed in Acland Street, St Kilda, hit by a cyclist as she began to cross the road. My wife, Yael, and I saw her lying on the road, blood coming from her ears. Yael and another bystander ran to the medical clinic she knew to be opposite where the woman lay. A doctor came, rested the poor woman's head on a cushion, loosened her clothes, examined her as best he could and arranged for an ambulance to come, but it did her little good. Three days later she died in hospital.

Only two or three people stopped to offer help. No more gathered out of curiosity. I wish I could say that people turned away deliberately from the woman lying on the road, made anxious perhaps by such a pitiable sight, or by the prospect of becoming emotionally entangled beyond their capacity to cope. But I cannot. There seemed not enough interest in the woman's fate for me to say that with confidence.

Gypsy is our German shepherd bitch. At the time she was two years old. A week after the old woman had been killed she and I

were standing on the footpath in Acland Street, waiting for Yael who was shopping in the supermarket. More than twenty minutes had passed and Gypsy was becoming anxious. We saw Yael at the same time thirty metres away. Foolishly I let Gypsy off the leash to run to her. Oblivious in her excitement to the many people on the footpath, she entangled herself under the feet of a huge, drunk man.

I saw it as though it happened in slow motion. Unable to understand what had happened to him, the drunk fell backwards, with hands and feet splayed as though falling from a height. Too drunk for his reflexes to do him or Gypsy any good, he didn't roll sideways, away from the living thing he must have dimly perceived to be underneath him. He crashed down on Gypsy and then rolled slowly away from her to pick himself up, stumbling as he did so and nearly crashing head first through a shop window.

Gypsy lay on her side on the footpath howling in agony. It was a terrible sound wrenched from the deepest part of her—almost too high-pitched to be called a howl, too strong and involuntary to be called a whine or a squeal. Yael ran to us as fast as the weight of the shopping she carried in both hands would allow her, eyes wide, brow pulled high and furrowed in distress. 'My God, what has happened here?' Phrased as a question it was in fact a lament. Her fatalism assured her of the worst.

I fear that it will sound frivolous, but I will say it anyhow because I'm sure that it played a considerable part in what happened next. Gypsy was an unusually good-looking dog. We could hardly walk twenty metres with her before someone would comment on her fine appearance—often it would be girls remarking on her beauty to their boyfriends. She had the bearing of a thoroughbred

for a dog?

shepherd and beautiful colouring—black and tan that merged into various shades of red—and she had an exceptionally pretty face, alert, with eyebrows that made her seem melancholy when her face was in repose. Yael is also beautiful. The two of them, Gypsy lying on the footpath and Yael kneeling beside her, the one howling and the other wailing from deep within her Jewish soul, made a bitter-sweet spectacle that proved irresistible to many passers by. Within a few minutes it had attracted a crowd of some twenty or thirty people.

First on the scene were two middle-aged Jewish women. They joined in the commotion. 'Oi veyh! The poor dog,' they intoned. Their sympathy, however, was not just for Gypsy. Although they didn't express it verbally, I could read the thought that was written all over their faces when they looked at Yael: 'That such a thing should happen to such a lovely Jewish girl.'

The poor drunk apologised abjectly, again and again. He was now focused just enough to know that, if the hullabaloo around him were any indication, he had been the cause of something terrible. His apologies made no impression on the two women, however. When they saw that the cause of all this trouble was drunk, their hearts hardened against him. The sight, smell and sound of drunken gentiles engaged in murderous pogroms have gone deep into the Jewish psyche. Contempt flashed so fiercely in their eyes that I feared for his safety. He must have done so too, because he sidled off as soon as the women's attention was drawn back to Gypsy and Yael.

Within minutes two passing motorists stopped at the same time to ask if they could take us to a vet. We accepted the first offer.

Gypsy needed an X-ray, the vet told us, but first she would be anaesthetised. It would cost seventy dollars. Quite a lot for a dog, I thought, as we went home to await the results due an hour or so later. Now that the drama had subsided we felt bewildered. Our attention was intensely focused on Gypsy, but we were haunted by the memory of the woman run down a week before, virtually neglected as she lay dying.

Gypsy's leg was not broken, but our relief at the news was short-lived. We had reason to wish her leg were broken, the vet told us, because her actual injury would prove more difficult and more expensive to fix. The surgery would be complicated and delicate. He recommended that we take her to the Melbourne University veterinary school at Werribee which had facilities and expertise greater than he could muster. Gypsy was visibly anxious when Yael and I took her there, as though seized by a sense of foreboding generated by our own anxiety.

At Werribee the surgeons planted a pin in Gypsy's leg and told us the prognosis was good. When we fetched her after the operation we expected that she would greet us with evident pleasure. Instead, she barely acknowledged us as she walked unsteadily towards us from the kennel where she had been recovering, her tail between her legs and her head low. With a bucket on her head to prevent her from chewing the plaster that encased her leg, she looked pitiful, entirely bereft of her youthful confidence.

Her despondency lasted only two days, however. Constant attention from Yael and me and from the children restored her spirits. On the third day, undeterred by the bucket on her head, she bit through her plaster. On the fourth she was back in Werribee for a second operation because she had injured her leg again.

Dismayed by the prospect that this might repeat itself indefinitely, I wondered what we should do if the vets had to amputate her leg. Should we put her down? The children were horrified at the thought. Had it come to a decision we couldn't have done it, I'm sure, but I'm ashamed to admit that I thought of it. Growing up with my father, I should have known better, for I learnt from him to be wary of the ease with which we judge that animals should be 'put out of their misery'. He kept his dog Russy alive for more than a year beyond the point where a vet suggested he should be put down. Neighbours who saw Russy said the same as the vet. Yet there was no evidence that he was in pain, or that he was unhappy. He was incapacitated and vividly a dog living beyond the term of 'his natural life', but living in a family with people devoted to his care was not part of his natural life either. The thought, common amongst my father's neighbours, that it would be a mercy to Russy if he were killed, seemed to have more to do with how much human beings were prepared to do for animals than with the state of the dog. Had my father not been prepared to feed him by hand, lift him onto the bed and keep him warm in the kitchen, then his life would have been a misery. But my father did all these things.

Yet it was only a year or so later, when I was in Virginia staying with the philosopher Cora Diamond, that I fully realised how shameful it was to have thought about Gypsy that way. Cora had a huge Beauceron dog called Mouse who had sustained an injury that had paralysed her hind legs. By pushing with her front legs, Mouse was able to move without much difficulty on a cart Cora had made for her. When Mouse needed to go outside, Cora would lift her gently by the hind quarters and then walk her on her front legs, at the angle of a wheelbarrow. No one could say Mouse would have been better off dead.

At the time when all this happened I was working in London, coming to Melbourne every university vacation. Maintaining two homes, paying airfares and sending children to private schools was impossible on my academic salary and the salary Yael earned as a schoolteacher. Yael's father had a stall at Victoria Market where he sold pullovers and shirts in winter and shirts and shorts in summer. He was a builder by trade, but kept the stall for when times were bad and because he enjoyed its convivial vitality. Seeing our need, he pretended that he was fed up with working the market and that he looked forward to retiring. The truth was that he wanted us to benefit from the extra income we would earn if we took over his stall. When we did that, he found himself another stall, at an inferior location on the fringes of the market where I believe he lost more money than he made.

Yael and I worked the market on weekends. When I was in London she did it herself. We arrived around five or six in the morning so that we could be set up by eight at the latest. Once set up, we looked forward to breakfast. Few things are so pleasurable as a junk-food breakfast—for us it was usually an egg and bacon roll and a cup of coffee—after setting up at the market on a cold winter's morning. The work isn't hard, but the hours are long, from five in the morning to five in the afternoon, and standing in the wind with the cold coming through the concrete into your bones

for a dog?

can be demoralising if you are not selling enough even to cover costs.

By now the cost of Gypsy's operations and other vet fees totalled more than two thousand dollars. Making only two or three dollars profit on a shirt at times, we tried, disconsolately, to estimate how many shirts we needed to sell in order to pay her vet bills. We had decided to work the market to make money to pay for school fees and repairs on the house. Instead we were working for a dog. How far would we go, I wondered, before I said, 'No more. This time she will have to be put down.' I had no idea, but I was reasonably confident that whatever answer I came to would be on the wrong side of what Yael and the children would find acceptable, and that, if it came to it, I would have to act against their tears. I recalled a man in England whose German shepherd became lost. He, the dog and his family achieved national fame when he declared on television that, having already spent thousands of pounds on a national advertising campaign, he was now prepared to sell the family home to raise more money to pay for more advertising and to increase still further the huge reward he was offering for the return of the dog. It seemed to me then, and still does, that he was someone who had wrongly accorded to a dog the value that is normally attached only to human beings. To pay for the children's medical expenses I would sell everything and work myself into the grave if I had to. But for a dog?

For a dog as opposed to what? A cat? A robot? Many people prefer cats to all other animals, but if they answered my question with, 'Not for a dog, but for a cat,' it could only be as a joke. Chimps and dolphins are reckoned by some people to be higher on the moral scale than cats or dogs, but I think that few of them would say, 'Not for a dog or a cat but for a chimp or a dolphin.' Or, if they did, they would say it polemically against the grain of the question. It's true that if we had been selling shirts to care for goldfish, then someone might say, 'For a cat or a dog I could understand. But for a fish?' Rats and gerbils are not likely to do much better. In the context in which I asked it, everyone would take the question to mean, 'For an animal?' Which would in turn be taken to mean, 'Aren't you treating your dog as though she were a human being?' To which someone might want to say, 'Human beings are animals too.'

More often than not, that would be a polemical retort, one that can generate controversies in which it is hard to see the wood for the trees. It has the form of a reminder, but of course no one has forgotten that human beings are also animals, creatures of flesh and blood, that our children grow in their mothers' wombs and are suckled at their breasts. Our understanding of the definitive facts of the human condition—our sexuality, our vulnerability to misfortune, our morality—is determined through and through by our creatureliness. Like other living creatures we die rather than break down. Ashes to ashes, dust to dust, rather than rusting or recycling, is the manner of our ending.

Often when people say that human beings are also animals, they mean to say that reference to the species to which a creature belongs can never of itself be a good reason for treating it one way or another. If it's absurd to think we should sacrifice as much for Gypsy as for our children, they say, it is not only because she is a dog and our children are human beings. It must be because of other objective differences between them which we take to be morally salient. There are plenty of differences between human beings and

for a dog?

dogs that justify treating human beings differently from dogs, and no doubt those differences are a function of their species membership, but, they insist, it is to those differences that one should appeal when justifying treating dogs and human beings differently rather than to the membership. To appeal merely to the fact that Gypsy is a dog to justify putting her down is to be guilty of 'speciesism', just as one is guilty of racism if one appeals merely to race or to colour, or sexism if one appeals merely to gender. Take anything whatsoever—an animal, a machine, an angel, an alien—if it has features and capacities that we regard as morally relevant in our treatment of human beings, then we should treat that thing as we treat human beings with those features and capacities. So runs a very influential argument. It appeals powerfully to our need for consistency.

Looking with reflective attention at the way we treat animals it would be understandable if we concluded that our behaviour towards them is noticeably inconsistent. The farmer's daughter will care tenderly for her pet lamb yet at the same time eat other lambs without hesitation; but that is just a dramatic manifestation of the common fact that we care for our pets and cheerfully eat other animals. We bury our pets yet run over dead creatures on the road with not much more than a wince. One could fill pages enumerating apparent inconsistencies of the same kind. Similar things, to be sure, mark our treatment of other human beings—the moral deformations of partiality, some would call them. Generally, however, when we are confronted with the partiality we show members of our family, or our nation, we respond at least to some degree to the demand that it should not conflict with obligations to faraway strangers and to other people to whom we have no attachments. Though our attachment may be profoundly local we acknowledge at least some obligations that are both expressive and constitutive of our sense of common humanity with all the peoples of the earth—obligations that are increasingly manifest in conceptions of human rights and international law, for example. Not much of that kind has transformed our relations to animals. We have felt little pressure to explain how we could care so much—sometimes so extravagantly—for our pets and so little for other animals.

Tosca, an attractive tabby cat, came with our house in St Kilda. She had never been fully domesticated and even before we got Gypsy she would seldom be coaxed into the house. Every so often, however, she would allow us—mostly Yael and Eva—to pat her. Occasionally she wanted to be patted. Then she would come into the house, leaving when she had had enough. On summer days, if Yael lay in the sun, Tosca would sometimes jump on her lap, purring, at first cautiously and then with as much abandonment as this street-wise cat could allow herself. We didn't know how old she was: about middle age, we reckoned, an estimate supported by her stubborn ways and her inclination to behave like a madam. When Gypsy was brought into the house as a nine-week-old pup, I encouraged her to be friendly to Tosca but my efforts came to nothing. As soon as she saw Tosca she struggled to free herself of my hold and the undistractable intensity of her gaze made her intention quite plain.

Soon after we got Gypsy it became evident that she was a killer. Many dogs chase cats, but some chase them with a determination that tells you straight away that they will kill them if they catch

for a dog?

them. Gypsy was a killer of most things. I'm reluctant to admit it because readers who are not familiar with animals probably won't understand and are likely to take against her. In fact, except for when she was a pup and rounded up the children and their friends, nipping their heels, she has been a most gentle dog with people—a real lady as Yael would say to her when Gypsy took food from her hands, working her mouth around Yael's fingers to ensure that her teeth would never graze them.

From the beginning she was affectionate, although a little aloof as shepherds tend to be, taking affection on her own terms. Until middle-aged, she could not take too much of it, though even then she liked always to be near to us. In the house most of the day, she slept in our bedroom at night. People say that large dogs need space. Gypsy needed space to run and she had it in the park and on the beach, but most of the time when we were home she sat with us and when we were out she slept in the house. She would have been happy enough in a small apartment, I think, provided we took her regularly for runs.

When she was just over a year old she became an effective watchdog, barking fearsomely as soon as she heard the click of the metal latch on the front gate, though only when we were in the house, it seems. 'This dog is not worth a cracker,' Yael's father said more than once because she didn't bark when he came to the house while we were away. We didn't know whether this was because she knew his step or whether she protected persons while having no regard for property. Though he was very fond of Gypsy and also a socialist, Yael's father gave no credence to the latter supposition. In any event, whenever I was away from the house at night—but only then—she barked at anything that moved, sensing that Yael and her daughters Dahlia and Michelle were in need of her protection. Despite the fact that Gypsy's constant barking kept them awake, she was a great comfort to them. When I returned she barked only when she heard the latch on the gate or sensed that someone was at the front or back door. A bitch in more ways than one, and a bit of a princess even into old age, her attitude to the protection of Yael and the children brought out the best in her. A dog of noble bearing, she rose to her responsibilities and became a noble dog.

Whenever she set eyes on Tosca, however, she seemed wholly savage, though Tosca paid little heed to the fact and was foolish with Gypsy. When Gypsy was inside the house, Tosca would provoke her by sitting in plain view on the window ledge outside, taking evident pleasure in seeing the dog go wild, knowing herself to be safe behind the glass. And such smug pleasure it was. But a middle-aged cat, even as street-wise as Tosca was, can do that for only so long to a young and clever shepherd with a killer instinct.

We all dreaded that Gypsy would kill Tosca one day, but none of us dreamed that she might do it with one leg in plaster and her head in a bucket. Eva saw it happen. Gypsy trapped Tosca at a fence from which she had fallen while trying to escape. By the time I responded to Eva's cries Gypsy had Tosca between her teeth and was shaking her to break her back.

Eva, then only nine years old, rushed bravely to rescue Tosca from Gypsy's jaws, was badly scratched by Tosca, and retreated. Nonetheless, Eva's intervention distracted Gypsy sufficiently for her to loosen her grip on Tosca, enabling her to escape. Yael caught Gypsy and held her.

for a dog?

Tosca crawled painfully to the back gate where she lay, blood trickling from her mouth, Her rib cage looked as though it had collapsed. Her eyes were wide open but seemed to be unseeing. I thought only of relieving her distress as soon as I could and looked for a shovel I knew to be in the yard. A quick hard hit and she would be dead. As I was looking, Yael called me to attend to Eva who was standing at the back door, her arm bloodied, crying partly because of her wounds and partly from shock. When I resumed my search for the shovel a couple of minutes later, Tosca was gone. Off to die, I thought. Cats do that.

A week or so later Yael thought she heard Tosca miaow, but said nothing to me, thinking it could not be true. A few days later she again thought she heard her, but this time she told me. 'It's impossible that Tosca could have survived such serious injuries,' I said.

Three weeks later Tosca came home. Or almost home. Yael heard her and, trusting her instinct that it was Tosca, found her under a bush by the side of the house. She was skin and bone and, because of the damage that Gypsy's jaws had done, her middle section was still partially caved in, causing her hind parts to sway in the opposite direction to her front and her miaow to sound strangulated and hoarse. We assumed that she had hidden under our neighbour's house and that, weak and injured though she was, she must have caught sufficient food to survive.

For about a year, it seemed that Tosca had been chastened by her scrape with death. Then she began to sit on the window sill again when Gypsy was in the room, though not at first in quite the same old smug way, for she was still a little nervous of what she was daring to do. Eventually, complacency set in. Gypsy caught her a second time. Again we rescued her from Gypsy's jaws and took her to the vet, where she survived for a night at the cost of one hundred dollars for accommodation plus treatment. I remember thinking that it would have been better if Gypsy had killed her outright. The vet disposed of her remains.

Of all of us, Yael was most upset. For three days she could barely speak to Gypsy. Though she didn't like cats, she became attached to Tosca because she fed her and because Tosca came to her more than to anyone else on the rare occasions she allowed someone to pat her. When she was little, Yael's three budgies were eaten by a cat and it set her against cats for life. People are like that. When children of friends, passionate cat lovers, heard that Gypsy had killed Tosca, they took against her even though I pointed out that their beloved cats had surely killed many birds. If truth be told, Tosca got her comeuppance. One might have wished it had not been so severe, but that is to place a human sense of proportion on what transpired between her and Gypsy. Tosca showed admirable spirit in that she should so soon after her resurrection tease Gypsy with such condescension, but it would be a denial of that same spirit to refuse to acknowledge that she paid the price for the deadly game she chose to play. Tosca had it coming, but Gypsy did not kill her because she had it coming. The thought never crossed her mind. Nothing crossed her mind. That, I suspect, is part of what it means to be an animal.

In later years, when I reflected on the fact that I searched for a shovel to crash on Tosca's head in order to 'put her out of her misery', I realised that I would never have done the same to Gypsy. Nor would I have left her dead for a vet to dispose of. I would have

for a dog?

buried her as my father buried Orloff. Even if I had no alternative but to take a shovel and kill her to relieve her of her suffering, I would have done it in a different spirit, one informed by the pained realisation that this really was the only thing left for me to do. But though I was pained at the prospect of having to kill Tosca, and though I took no pleasure in the way I chose to do it, I set out to do it obedient to the instinct of someone who had grown up on a farm. That is what one did on a farm. The thought that one should do it in only the most desperate of circumstances played no part in farm life. That fact and others like it give the connotations that attach to our use of the expressions 'putting an animal out of its misery' and 'putting an animal down'.

My awareness of the brutishness of what I had intended to do to Tosca had nothing to do with my estimate of whether it would have been painful for her. I assumed that if I had hit her with sufficient force I would not have caused her pain. Our attention, when we think about these matters, is too easily drawn to what the animal will feel and we think too little of what our actions mean. We think about the pain we will cause but not the dishonour we will inflict. To see the difference one need only reflect on how desperate the circumstances would have to be before one would consider killing a human being by crashing a shovel onto her head, and how terrible it would be to do it no matter what the circumstances and no matter whether one thought (rightly or wrongly) that they justified it.

Again, this is not because she might suffer pain, mental or physical—but because it would be an assault on her dignity. If she were conscious, then any adequate characterisation of her anguish at the prospect of being killed in this way would need to be informed, through and through, by that fact. In the case of human beings the dignity and the respect owed are not the kind, for example, appealed to by people who insisted, during World War I that officers should be shot rather than 'hanged as common criminals'. It is respect of the kind we call unconditional. It is owed to human beings as such, whatever their standing or status, and whatever their merit.

The spirit in which I intended to kill Tosca is caught in the associations that have accrued to the expressions 'putting an animal out of its misery' and 'putting an animal down'. Neither just means killing a being in order to relieve it of further suffering. Only someone who is tone-deaf could think either to be an apt description of euthanasia. Otherwise, jokes about putting down one's granny would not strike us as black humour. We apply these expressions only to the killing of animals, thus marking a difference in kind between compassion that is properly shown to animals and compassion that is properly shown to human beings. It is one aspect of the way we mark the difference between animals and human beings—between us and them. To Tosca, when I intended to kill her, I showed the former kind of compassion. It would not be so with Gypsy.

Was I wrong to intend to kill Tosca that way? I think I was. Should I extend to all animals the kind of compassion I would extend to Gypsy, respectful of their dignity in the way that is not consistent with 'putting them out of their misery'? Am I wrong even to ask that question? Should the answer not be obvious now? I think it's not obvious. But it is obvious that it would be outrageous to think that, though one wouldn't put one's own granny down, it might be all right for others to do it, or for one to do it for others.

for a dog?

One day—and it may not be too far away—we may look with revulsion at the cruelty of many of our current practices in relation to animals. But we may also become deeply ashamed of how impoverished our sense was of animal dignity. We may become incredulous that we could ever have left animal corpses on the road to be run over again and again. If we do, we may come—indeed I am sure that we will come—to see that revulsion as emerging consistently from the more 'humane' of our present practices. But our sense of why we should not distinguish so radically between individual animals or between kinds of animals will not, I think, show that we have come to believe that the difference between them does not justify the different ways we treat them.

When I reflected critically on my response to Tosca I didn't consciously—or, I believe, unconsciously—think there were no salient points of difference between her and Gypsy or, more generally, between cats and dogs. And I know full well that the dog left dead by the side of the road has the same objective characteristics as Gypsy. True, we do not think of behaving towards goldfish or insects in the way we behave towards our cats and dogs, but I suspect it is not their objective differences in themselves that matter to us so much as the relations those features make possible for us. Even then, the features themselves never fully explain the relations they make possible. Gypsy is a member of the family. Some people baulk at that description, thinking that it should be put in inverted commas under pain of sentimentality. Others do not. Nothing objective about German shepherds will settle the matter.

Years after her accident, when Gypsy was ten years old, she was involved in a serious fight with another German shepherd bitch who was much younger and had all the power of youth. The other dog's sister hovered uncertainly on the sidelines. No one knew whether she would join in on the side of her sister. It was a savage fight. Bitches will more often fight to the death than male dogs, and this fight looked as if it might turn out that way. I tried to separate them. I grabbed the attacking dog by the collar and attempted to lift her off Gypsy, who was getting the worst of it, but she twisted and turned so powerfully that she threw me off with a torn ligament in my shoulder. Seeing what had happened, Yael moved in to separate the snarling combatants, with the other dog circling her, excited but still uncommitted. She grabbed the younger dog's tail and pulled it hard. She kicked her in the backside and kept pulling and kicking until the dog withdrew. Without doubt it was a brave thing to do. No one could be sure the two other shepherds would not turn on her. Yael could have been seriously injured, or even killed. Again I wondered: for a dog?

The Philosopher's Dog

When Gypsy lies on her mat in the kitchen, her head resting on her crossed paws, looking vacantly into the middle distance, and we are at the table, eating or just talking after the meal, I sometimes wonder what goes on inside her head. Is she thinking anything? I imagine there is hardly anyone whose dog has become part of the family, living inside the house, who has not asked that question. It seems irresistible, which is strange, because I'm quite sure she doesn't think anything. Why then do I—why do so many people— ask that question? Because, I think, we are struck every so often by the mystery of animals, their otherness to us and to our lives. A long history of philosophical and scientific reflection has made it seem natural to express that mystery as being about animal consciousness. It's natural, but I believe it's mistaken.

Teaching Gypsy to sit on her mat was an aspect of teaching her to become a member of the family. When we bought her as a nine- week-old pup, her breeders called her mother into the house to demonstrate this to us. Once we had admired her—with some reservation because she had a floppy left ear that we feared she might have passed on to Gypsy—she was told to sit on her mat, which she did with impressive matter-of-factness. Her owner advised us to teach Gypsy (or Elsa as she was then called) to do the same if we intended to allow her into the house for any length of time. He would advise it for any dog, he said, but especially for Gypsy because she had already proved a handful. Full of cheek and mischief as she was, he predicted she would be determined to get her own way. It proved to be so.

Learning to sit on her mat when she is asked or commanded to—she responds differently according to which it is—is a lesson Gypsy generalises to rugs in other parts of the house. Our insistence that she learn it was part of disciplining her. Throw the idea of disciplining a dog into a random group of people and they will, I suspect, divide into two. The view of the majority will be informed by the idea that a dog is a mechanical bundle of stimulus response mechanisms, or perhaps that together with exploitable instincts. And there will be those infused with the hope that a dog might be educated into citizenship, as Vicki Hearne puts it (with only a little of her tongue in her cheek) in her marvellous book *Adam's Task: Calling Animals by Name.*

Though she writes with some humour about this, Hearne is serious in suggesting that we should apply, even to dogs, the idea that freedom is obedience to necessity rather than freedom from it. The distinction marks an old argument in political philosophy and Hearne reckons the relation between some owners and their highly disciplined working dogs shows a freedom of a different kind than is enjoyed by wild animals—a kind that is better conceptualised by analogy with the freedom that law and obedience to it makes possible in human affairs. She knows, of course, that the analogy holds only if there exist between human beings and their dogs (and other animals) relations of the kind that enable us to distinguish a command issued with rightful authority from an act of force. She thinks these do exist, and writes impressively about them in a chapter entitled 'Teaching a Dog to Fetch'. She shows that one must earn a right to command a dog, and that possession of the right depends on earning and deserving the dog's respect.

Hearne is more right than wrong, I think, though I am sure that many people will think that she is over the top. Reflection might bring some of them who have seen fine sheepdogs at work to the realisation that the discipline that enables them to perform so impressively enhances rather than diminishes their freedom. The point, however, is not so much that disciplining a dog unlocks potentialities and enables the dog to fulfil them, in much the same way that disciplining children does. True and important though that is, it doesn't get to the heart of Hearne's insight which is that freedom is constituted by certain kinds of moral relations, rather than simply enabled and enhanced by them. It exists only when there is respect for an animal's dignity in addition to concern for its welfare. Or, to put it better, it exists only when a concern for its welfare is transformed by respect for its dignity. Forgetful of this, we are not only cruel to animals and forgetful of their needs. We also degrade them.

As with human beings, respect for an animal's dignity goes together with expectations of it that are naturally called moral. We expect Gypsy not to bite the guests, let alone any of the family.

When she was younger we expected her to defend members of the family. We don't just predict these things as a consequence of her training. In fact, she wasn't trained if one takes that to mean that we subjected her to a program of conditioning. Nothing we did in teaching her the ways of family living was informed by that (behaviouristic) way of thinking of her and of her relations to us. Like Hearne, I believe nothing much would get done if behaviouristically minded animal trainers fully practised what they preach. Instead, those instincts of a pack animal Gypsy brought to living together with us were transformed (humanised, I would say) under that discipline, enabling her to participate to some degree in a human form of life. Her obedience cannot, in my judgment, be characterised adequately either by stimulus response theories, or by reference to how she would have responded to the 'top dog' in a pack, or by some combination of both.

So we did not discipline Gypsy to make her predictable. We did it to make her trustworthy. It takes courage for a dog to attack a strange human being in order to defend members of its family. A dog who has never been required to curb her desires is unlikely to curb a desire to run away rather than stand her ground. We trust Gypsy to do certain things and not others. And if our trust should turn out to be ill-founded, we will feel let down. Were it to happen, I believe she would know it.

When I stand on Gypsy's paw and she howls, I have no doubt that she is in pain. Nor do I doubt that when I cuddle her and apologise she is comforted, relieved that I expressed no hostile intent. Sometimes she thinks that her food is coming when it is not. She hopes to go for walks and plays games in which she tries to trick me into thinking she will run this way when she intends to run the other. Occasionally she sulks when I reprimand her. An intelligent dog, she is not a wise one. She has both character and personality. Her character is in part that of her breed—'steady of nerve, self-assured, courageous and tractable, never nervous, overly aggressive or shy' according to the Kennel Club Breeders Association of Great Britain. She is sensitive (though not to the degree that Zac was) to our moods and feelings and is herself sometimes joyful, miserable, depressed and bored. She is also mischievous, cheeky, stubborn, a bit of a princess and always on the lookout for opportunities to get her way with strangers who come to the house. When the cleaning lady comes, we know that some mischief will have been done because Gypsy knows that she can get the better of her. There will be a hole dug, or the hose will be bitten through or there will be yet more teeth marks on the vacuum cleaner.

Were I not sure of most of these and like things, and were not Yael and the children sure of them, we could not think of Gypsy as part of the family. Some of what I have said will provoke scepticism, I know. One might justifiably wonder what I can mean by saying that Gypsy responds to my apology. Do I think she possesses the concept of an apology? I'm sure she doesn't, but I'm sure that when I cuddle her after I have accidentally hurt her, she knows I didn't mean to hurt her and (I think) that I am sorry that I did.

On occasion, of course, I am wrong. When Gypsy pricks up her ears, sits up and then runs to the back door, I might think she believes Yael is coming home whereas she might believe that the neighbour's dogs are out the back. And sometimes I have no idea what is going on. Then I might conjecture that she thinks this or that. Sometimes I might never know. But I don't *conjecture* whether she is the kind of creature who is sometimes warm and sometimes cold, who sometimes has pleasures and is sometimes in pain, who sometimes believes one thing and hopes or fears another. Nor do I *assume* it, or *take it as certain*—that is, for practical though not for philosophical or scientific purposes. I am absolutely certain, that is to say, I have not the slightest doubt. I am equally certain that when she lies on her mat or sits at the front door gazing out to sea, she is not thinking of her sins or of the problems of philosophy.

No one, of course, who is uncertain about these things, or who is certain but thinks it reasonable to doubt, will be impressed by my certainty, for I have given no evidence to support it. Surely, I must know that much of what I have said about Jack, Orloff, Zac and Gypsy is highly controversial. Yet I have given no justification for my certainty.

It is true: I gave no evidence that when Gypsy lay on the footpath howling she was howling with pain, nor evidence that Jack was affectionate to my father when he climbed into his bed and put his beak to his lips, nor that he was cold when he sat wet and shivering on the chair that Hora placed in front of the fire. Nor did I provide evidence that Gypsy sometimes accepts that I did not mean to hurt her, or that sometimes she believes Yael is coming home. I was dismissive of the suggestion that Zac was really after the salt in Eva's tears. Most astonishing of all was my confession that I have moral expectations of Gypsy and that it would have dishonoured

Tosca to hit her with a shovel in the spirit of putting her out of her misery.

These are, to be sure, a mixed bag of examples. Some are more controversial than others. Few people would ask why I am sure that Gypsy was howling in pain when the drunk crashed on her leg. But nor would many people ask me to justify why I believed that Zac was showing tender concern for Eva rather than enjoying the salt in her tears, or that Gypsy thought Yael was coming home. Those who are sceptical about Zac and Eva or about Gypsy and Yael would ask why I believe that dogs could *ever* show tender concern or believe anything. Why then do they not ask why I am certain that Gypsy is a sensate creature? Is it because it is obvious that she is?

Many people, I think, believe that it is so obvious that it would be silly to ask for evidence. No one seriously doubts that dogs are sensate creatures, they will say. I think it's true that no one seriously doubts this, but I think it is not true that this is because it's obvious, or because the evidence for it is overwhelming. In a class—perhaps a philosophy class inquiring into what we know and how we know it, into the degree of justified confidence we can have for the various kinds of things we claim to know—what would someone put forward to show that we had evidence to overwhelm anyone who professed seriously to doubt that dogs are sensate creatures? Their behaviour, presumably, and perhaps some facts about their nervous system, although it's important to acknowledge that, with respect to the latter, most of us know virtually nothing, nor do we think we need to know anything in order to be absolutely certain that dogs are sensate creatures. Knowledge of a dog's nervous system would add not the slightest to our certainty; it might tell us a lot about dog sensations, but it can play no role in convincing us that dogs have sensations. To try to make it play that role would be like smashing a stone to pieces in order to prove that, because it has no nervous system, we are now completely justified in our certainty that stones don't hurt when we kick them.

Yet, in such a class, an obvious question would be raised. How can we be certain—just from observing the dog's behaviour, which we can see—that it has sensations which we cannot see? Grant that we are certain, could we not, just for the sake of argument, ask whether the dog's behaviour justifies that certainty? The classical answer to that question, once it has been raised, either about human beings or animals, is a sceptical one. There is always some distance between the behaviour and what we take it to prove. Some people say the distance is small. They say we can be almost certain, so that for all intents and purposes we can act as though there is no doubt. We can perhaps be 99 per cent certain. Philosophers, they say, may bother about the 1 per cent, but it won't trouble ordinary people getting on with their lives. And when philosophers leave their studies or classrooms and are again ordinary people getting on with their lives, then it doesn't bother them either. The great eighteenth-century Scottish philosopher David Hume, who raised many radical doubts concerning what we can be sure of, said that his doubts dissipated when they were overtaken by the pleasures of convivial conversation with his friends over a game of backgammon.

When philosophers respond to the problem of scepticism, to the question of whether there are minds other than their own, then those who admit that they cannot satisfactorily answer the sceptic tend to fall back on some version of the distinction between what a pure mind, purged of everyday prejudices and the demands of practical life, might find doubtful—can doubt at least in principle—and what we ordinary human beings can actually doubt. In order to explain why the doubt does not explode into ordinary life—why conversation and backgammon can so easily put the philosophical mind at rest—the most favoured answer is that philosophical standards of certainty are unnaturally fastidious and the grounds for doubts are not so great. That, we are told, is why we can accept the 99 per cent option.

It looks rigorous but really its rigour is ersatz. The 99 per cent option is intended to reconcile conflicting appearance—that the doubt over the existence of other minds is real and that no one seriously doubts that there are other minds. But on what rational grounds are such probabilities calculated? There are none, I think. Once the doubt is raised, nothing can allay it. Or, more accurately, once we ask for evidence we will find none that is adequate to our certainty.

The distinction between something doubtful to reason purified of the dross of human living and something that human beings living a normal life are actually able to doubt has been crucial to the formulation of radical scepticism. Perhaps the best example of it occurs in René Descartes' wonderful little book, *Meditations on First Philosophy*. He writes that he is in his study sitting by the fire and recalls that sometimes he has dreamt that he is in his study sitting by the fire. How can he now know that he is not dreaming this? He reviews certain criteria whose application might enable him to know whether he is dreaming or awake, until the idea startles him that he may be dreaming they are criteria and that he is applying them. To his astonishment, he tells us, he realises 'that there are never any sure signs by means of which being awake can be distinguished from being asleep.'

It is a marvellous argument—simple, elegant and apparently free of contestable assumptions. It is not hard to imagine someone who is impressed by Descartes' argument, who writes it on a blackboard, becomes convinced of the truth of its premises and of the validity of the moves between them, and yet thinks that the conclusion is crazy. How, he asks, can anyone seriously conclude, in the ordinary circumstances of life, that she may be dreaming? He decides that, elegant and persuasive though the argument is, something *must* be wrong with it. He tries to find the fault, but to his embarrassment he fails. With mounting anxiety, he reviews the argument again and again, but cannot find fault with it. He is tired and agitated, he thinks. Tomorrow, with a clear head and calm spirit, he will try again, but the next day he fails once more.

What is the poor man to do? Take it from me, he is not being frivolous. Scepticism takes one to the deepest problems of human thinking. Philosophy, he believes, really matters. It is not just an intellectual game. Zeno's paradox, which allegedly proves that there is no such thing as motion, never interested him. He knew it was a mere puzzle. But Descartes' argument that we cannot know for certain that we are not dreaming is no mere puzzle. And this disciple, who writes it on the blackboard finding its conclusion inescapable and crazy, is committed with his whole being to the life of the mind. Now his mind—his reason—tells him he must accept the conclusion that he might at any time be dreaming. He is too serious to accept the 99 per cent option, knowing the comfort it offers is without foundation. He is torn apart. With his whole being, not just his mind abstracted from his humanity, he believes he must doubt. And with his whole being, not just with his humanity overriding his reason, he knows he cannot.

Should we then say that we *just know* that we are awake, or that dogs are sensate creatures? Not I think if we offer that as a response to the sceptic while accepting as exhaustive his division between absence of doubt that is justified and absence of doubt that is a mere psychological phenomenon. Offering that we just know there are other minds or that we are awake as self-evident warrant for the fact that we don't doubt these things is, I think, worthless. In the absence of an independent account of the faculty that so marvellously assures us that our certainty is justified, no mere psychological phenomenon, one may as well, as children sometimes do, stamp our feet to declaim our virtue.

Are we then just tawdry epistemic beings, as a philosopher once described us, who (perhaps for good evolutionary reasons) allow psychology to fill the holes left by critical reason, substituting a mere incapacity to doubt for warranted certainty? What an ignoble position that would be.

Does it matter? Are these not things of concern only to philosophers? Perhaps Callicles was right when he said to Socrates that, though philosophy is a noble pursuit in the young, an older person who is occupied with it needs a whipping. It does matter and Callicles was wrong. But even if scepticism about the existence of other minds is in the pejorative sense of interest only to philosophers, we who are interested in understanding our relations to animals need the right account of why we cannot doubt that dogs are sensate creatures. If we do not have it we will get into trouble when we come to think about why we are (or should be) certain that dogs do not think about higher mathematics. Because they have a flawed understanding of this, many people who are quite untroubled by their incapacity to doubt that dogs are sensate are driven to say, with more than a little embarrassment, that in the end we cannot be sure what dogs think about. They have their own, but equally bad, version of the 99 per cent option. We are 99 per cent certain, they say, that Gypsy doesn't think about mathematics or about the day's events as she sits on her mat gazing out to sea. Nor, we are 99 per cent sure, does she wonder whether she should refuse to steal from the rubbish tin because it is intrinsically wrong rather than because she fears a scolding.

There is a better way. Perhaps, as Ludwig Wittgenstein suggested, we should cease to look for a justification while at the same time refusing to concede that this is intellectual dereliction. Perhaps we should look more closely at the big assumption, shared by the sceptic and those who try to refute him, that the unhesitating responses that express our certainty are based on beliefs. I respond to Gypsy howling, they say, *believing* her to be in pain, and I *believe* she is now in pain because I also *believe* she is a sensate creature. The same is true of our certainty that other human beings have minds. Belief here need not be contrasted with knowledge. When I say I know rather than merely believe, I am saying that my belief has a certain kind of justification. Even when I say I *just know*, without offering evidence, acknowledging that whatever evidence I have is weak, then, according to this assumption, I am nonetheless claiming to be cognitively related to what is there, to a state of affairs, or to some fact. The connection is sometimes called intuition, conceived to be a faculty of the mind. There is dispute about what can be intuited, but that we know that we are in pain when we are in pain is a classical contender. *You* might need evidence from my behaviour, but *I* just know it (by intuition, or by introspection). When philosophers, haunted by scepticism, try to provide a list of things that are known for certain, then that example is at the very top.

Even this Wittgenstein found suspect. When one is in pain, he said in *Philosophical Investigations*, one cannot say, except perhaps as a joke, that one *knows* that one is in pain. That seemed so outrageous to many philosophers that they thought he couldn't really mean it. They thought he meant that one couldn't normally say it—say it in the sense of *assert* it, intending to give someone information—because it is so obvious that if one is in pain one must know it. But Wittgenstein meant it. One couldn't even cite it as an example, in discussions of scepticism, of something one could know for certain, he said. Not because one could doubt it, but rather because nothing was added to the fact that one couldn't doubt it by saying that one couldn't doubt it *because* one knew it. Saying one knows (by introspection, or by intuition) creates the illusion that one has provided justified grounds for the fact that one cannot doubt it. 'One can't doubt that one is in pain because one knows it' (by means of some special epistemic faculty) is, Wittgenstein thought, an example of a pseudo-epistemological proposition. Say that one cannot doubt it and leave it at that, he suggested.

It's a radical thought, to be sure, one of the most radical ever to appear in philosophy. Whatever is finally to be said for it, it merits consideration, and therefore exposes as itself doubtful the assumption that constitutes the basis of scepticism and also the unsatisfactory responses to it. It proposes not an answer to scepticism, but its dissolution and with it the contrast between what is doubtful to purified reason and what as a mere fact cannot be doubted by creatures like us.

Almost all philosophical and scientific work about animals is based on the assumption that Wittgenstein threw into doubt—that we are justified in attributing various 'states of consciousness' to animals only to the degree that we have evidence for them. The picture that informs that assumption is exactly the same picture that informs scepticism more generally. It is that we are spectators in the world, incorrigibly aware of our own states through introspection, but corrigibly assuming the same states in others. When we become reflective spectators, we realise that assumptions about others must be questioned if we are to rise to our potential as rational beings. Each attribution then becomes a hypothesis, to be confirmed or rejected on the basis of the evidence.

People who cannot take seriously scepticism about the existence of other human minds are nonetheless ready to be seriously sceptical about animal minds. Many, I suspect, take the fact that we speak to one another, that we live in a world bathed in speech, as an implicit refutation of scepticism of other human minds even if, as would normally be the case, they could not explain why. But, they say, animals cannot tell us what is inside their heads. That is why we will never know. They will always be mysterious to us.

Sitting on Her Mat
Gazing Out to Sea

When she was five my daughter Katie complained to me of a pain in her stomach. Questioning proved it wasn't so bad, so I said, 'I have a pain too.'

'Where?' she asked.

'In my pocket,' I replied.

Without hesitation she responded, 'Don't be silly. You can't have a pain in your pocket.'

The immediacy of her response and its firmness excited my curiosity. What had started as merely an idle game promised some philosophical interest.

'How do you know I can't have a pain in my pocket. You now have a pain in your stomach. At other times you've had it in your head or in your legs. Well, I've had pains there too and in other places, including, now, my pocket. I've heard of other people who have pains in thin air, near to their bodies. Phantom limbs, they are called.'

None of this made an impression. 'You're being silly,' she insisted and she kept insisting it even after I admonished her for being dogmatic, for not being prepared to learn from others and their experiences.

'You're only five,' I said. 'How would you know where pains can be? Be open to experience. Learn from others. The world is filled with strange things.' Or words to that effect.

Katie wasn't an exceptionally sceptical child. Like most other children she believed in Santa Claus and the Easter Bunny. And at the same time as I was trying to convince her to be open to learning about where pains might be, she participated with me in an elaborate conceit, which lasted for a couple of years. I had told her that in a cake shop near King's College London, I had met a Lion and that we fell to talking about things, including the trouble he and his friend Hippopotamus were having with their teeth since Lion discovered this cake shop and brought cakes home to the zoo for them to share. His name, I said, was Lion-in-the-Cakeshop. My story started off as a simple morality tale to convince her always to brush her teeth, but it soon became elaborate and took on a life of its own. Lion (I told her) sometimes went to Africa with Hippopotamus, and because of our growing friendship he took an interest in Katie. From Africa he sent her pictures of himself with friends. He even telephoned regularly to see how she was and to tell her of his adventures.

Whether she believed this or merely participated in a fantasy, suspending disbelief, I cannot say. More the latter than the former, I suspect. Though she was only five, she was sufficiently intelligent and knowledgeable to ask why there seemed to be only one such

sitting on her mat gazing out to sea

lion in the world. But she didn't, and when she finally announced that there was no Lion-in-the-Cakeshop, it seemed quite different from her declaration that there was no Santa Claus.

Why was Katie so certain one could not have a pain in one's pocket, unmoved by my appeal that she should be more open to what the world might teach her? When we explain how we know what people feel, how and where they feel it, we sometimes appeal to our experiences, to what we have seen, heard or introspected. Sometimes we appeal to what we know by virtue of our place in a community in which people have authority. Science teaches us, we say, or it is common knowledge and has been so since time immemorial, or we have it on the authority of a priest or a guru. This is knowledge of the world secured by experience. If Katie's certainty that one can't have a pain in one's pocket were of that kind, then it would have been vulnerable to my responses to her. But it wasn't. Nor is my certainty that Gypsy does not think about her sins or the problems of philosophy, or that stones don't hurt when I kick them, or that frogs don't turn into princes.

There are of course things we know about pain which we have learnt through experience. We learn through introspective attention how to describe our pains, that they sometimes appear to migrate, that they can occur in the place where an arm had been but is no longer, and, of course, one learns about their physiological basis. We hear stories; we read scientific papers or summaries of them and so on. But that no one can have a pain in his pocket, or that no one can be in great pain without being aware of it, or that no one can post her pain to her doctor for scrutiny—these are not empirical generalisations secured by introspection of one's own pains or by reflection on the introspective reports of others. In rejecting so categorically the prima-facie authority of her father's claim to have an experience contrary to what she had thought was possible, she showed instinctively that she knew her denial did not rest upon an empirical generalisation. Nor was her certainty based on her introspection of her own pains. How could introspection of the features of our sensations justify such a categorical assertion that something was impossible?

There are cranks who believe the Earth is flat, that Elvis Presley is alive and working for the CIA or that they can read their future in coffee grounds. We call them cranks because they lack the kind of judgment that enables them rationally to draw conclusions from evidence. There are no cranks who believe that it is possible to have a pain in one's pocket. That is why Katie rejected not only my claim that I had a pain in my pocket, but also my protestations that I believed it. Only a very small child, considerably younger than Katie was, could even think it, and then only inchoately, for, as Katie's example shows, one could think it only if one had failed in quite fundamental ways to have mastered the concept of pain. But someone who has failed so fundamentally to master the concept of pain is in no position to have beliefs, true or false, about pain.

How then did Katie learn that one cannot have a pain in one's pocket? For learn it she did. She learnt it through learning to speak. Were the concept of a concept, and the distinction between beliefs and concepts, not so difficult and riddled with controversy, I would say that it belongs to the concept of a pain that it cannot be in one's pocket. And anyhow, some concepts store accumulated and established empirical knowledge. But it is surely not plausible that over many centuries humanity discovered and then firmly established that pain could not be in one's pocket. Or discovered that we cannot send our pain to someone else. Sitting in one and the same chair that you sat in, I discover that I have the same pain that you had. But I do not, in the same sense, discover that it is literally one and the same pain, which you felt yesterday and today has migrated to me.

It looks therefore as if there is an important difference between learning that pain comes and goes, that tablets can sometimes relieve it, that it is often connected with injury, that damage to some parts of the body can make one insensate, and learning that pain cannot be in one's pocket. The impossibility that is expressed when one says that one cannot have sensations when one's nervous system is damaged in certain ways is different from the kind of impossibility expressed when one says that one cannot have a pain in one's pocket. They are not two forms of the same kind of impossibility except that the latter is more firmly established. For the former it makes sense to ask for evidence and even if only a crank would doubt it one could still trace the historical accumulation of evidence until it became first conclusive, and then so well established as to be beyond rational doubt. But it makes no sense to review the historical accumulation of evidence that puts it beyond rational doubt that stones do not feel pain. Despite what people say about animism, nothing in our intellectual history—full of religious belief, myth and superstition—suggests we have moved from the belief that perhaps stones have pains to the certainty now that they don't.

Our incapacity to doubt that other human beings and animals are sensate is more like Katie's incapacity to take seriously my plea that she be open to the possibility that I had a pain in my pocket than to our incapacity to take seriously the claim that the Earth is flat or that, until recently, Elvis worked for the CIA.

In one of the most radical passages in the history of philosophy, Wittgenstein reflects:

> 'I believe that he is suffering'—Do I also believe that he isn't an automaton...
>
> 'I believe that he is not an automaton', just like that, so far makes no sense.
>
> My attitude towards him is an attitude towards a soul. I am not of the *opinion* that he has a soul.

Nothing should be read into Wittgenstein's use of the word 'soul' (*seele*). He means nothing more than a being with thoughts and feelings. He means an inner life, to be sure, but not as we mean it when we speak of an inner life with deeper and shallower possibilities. His point is that generally I cannot doubt that others are sentient beings, but that is not because I know they are. Behaviour (together with the circumstances of its occurrence) counts as evidence for the existence of a person's psychological states only against the background that (in normal circumstances) no one could seriously doubt that she is a human being with thoughts and feelings. It may help us to see Wittgenstein's point if we think of 'attitude' (*Einstellung*) in one of its older meanings, as when one speaks of the attitude of a compass needle. Think of us as inflected, so to speak, in interacting responses to the forms of the living body's expressiveness. Or better, think as the English philosopher Peter Winch suggested, of Marlene Dietrich singing 'Falling in Love Again' in which the German lyric goes: '*Ich bin*

sitting on her mat gazing out to sea

von Kopf zu Fuss auf Liebe, eingestellt' ('I'm all set for love from head to foot'). Out of such *'einstellungs'* we develop the concepts that mark the various forms of consciousness, including the concepts of belief and certainty.

One must be careful not to treat the unhesitating acknowledgment of others as based on an assumption that they have minds. Assumptions invite questions about whether they are justified. The trouble with this is not that under sceptical probing they might prove not to be. Even if we answer confidently and with justification that the assumption is correct, in doing so we stand on common ground with the sceptic in thinking that our unhesitating certainty is the kind of cognitive achievement that he is looking for but suspects cannot be given. In doing that, in thinking we can stand on the same ground and refute the sceptic—and there is no other ground on which something *will count as a refutation*—we distort the role that our behaviour plays in our understanding of ourselves and other people. 'What gives us so much as the idea that living beings, things, can feel?' Wittgenstein asks. His answer is that nothing gives us so much as the idea, for it is not a matter of having an idea. It is not an assumption, a conjecture, or a belief, or even knowledge.

Following Wittgenstein, Peter Winch calls many of the forms of an attitude towards a soul 'primitive reactions'. In his essay *'Eine Einstellung zur Seele'*, reprinted in his book *Trying to Make Sense*, he argues that these reactions are a condition rather than a consequence of ascribing states of consciousness to others. Such reactions—a variety of interacting responses to the demeanours of the human form—are partly constitutive of those concepts with which we describe the forms of bodily expressiveness—groans, smiles, grimaces and so on. They are the concepts with which we describe what we ordinarily call 'behaviour', all the subtle inflexions we bring under the notion of 'body language', and which distinguish behaviour from 'colourless bodily movement'. Binding a person's wound while looking into his face is an example of an attitude towards a soul. Wittgenstein's radical remark turns on its head the almost irresistibly natural thought that we react to others as to persons—as to 'other minds'—because we know, believe, or conjecture that they have psychological states more or less as we do.

Wittgenstein's remarks are about the responses of human beings to one another, but there is every reason to believe that exactly the same point applies to the responses of human beings to animals and (to a limited degree) their responses to us. There is no reason to think we form the concept of intention, for example, first in its application to human behaviour and that we then apply it to animals, when, for example, we see a dog running after a cat. That is what is assumed when people speak of anthropomorphism—that we illegitimately apply to animals concepts of conscious states that we have legitimately developed in relation to human beings. But such concepts, I have suggested, are formed in responses to animals and to human beings together. That is the deepest reason why it is not anthropomorphic to say that Gypsy intends this, or that she believes or hopes that.

When dogs respond to our moods, to our pleasures and fears, when they anticipate our intentions, or wait excitedly to see whether we will take them for a walk, they do not assume that we are sensate

sitting on her mat gazing out to sea

beings with intentions. I imagine that it was the same for us in our primitive state. Out of such unhesitating interactions, between ourselves, and between us and animals, there developed—not beliefs, assumptions and conjectures about the mind—but our *very concepts* of thought, feeling, intention, belief, doubt and so on. Misunderstanding this, captivated by a picture of ourselves as spectators, certain about our own minds, but driven to hypothesising about whether there may be other minds, we have misconstrued the natural history of the development of our concept of the mind. We have constructed the fiction that at a certain point of intellectual development we had to step back from our assumption that others have minds and to seek evidence for it. Only then, we think, did we make ourselves worthy hosts to the gift of reason. It is an edifying narrative, but it is, I believe, fiction.

The sceptic is half-right. Gypsy's howling in Acland Street provides no evidence to justify the complete absence of doubt that she is a sensate creature. Nor does anything else. But he is wrong to conclude that our certainty is insufficiently grounded, no matter how refined our intellectual purposes, because that presupposes that it should be well grounded. Her howling provides evidence that she was in terrible pain. But it provides evidence only because there is no room for serious doubt whether she is a sensate creature. Should someone doubt that, then her howling and the howling of a million dogs could not convince him. And it is no different with human beings. I could see the awful pain in the face of the woman lying in Acland Street and I heard it in her voice, but should a question arise as to whether she or any other human being except myself feels sensation, then all the expressiveness of body and voice would mean nothing to me. Our certainty is without evidence—*completely without evidence*—and is none the worse for that.

What then is the mystery I alluded to when I said that sometimes when I look at Gypsy sitting on her mat gazing out to sea I am struck by the mysterious otherness of her? Why did I then deny that I am struck by the mystery of animal consciousness?

'Consciousness' is a word to make mischief with. If there is a mystery of consciousness, it is the metaphysical mystery of how there could be such a thing in a material world. But, as I have often said, I have no doubt that Gypsy sometimes thinks her food is coming, that she hopes to go for a walk, that she is sometimes happy and sometimes miserable. If the word 'consciousness' means anything then I have no doubt that Gypsy is a conscious being. I am equally sure that she is not a reflective being. About some other things, I am uncertain. I don't know if she deliberates about means to ends, for example, but the uncertainty prompts nothing more in me than a calm shrug of the shoulders. Nothing about which I concede uncertainty appears to account for the mystery. For me the mystery is not the mystery of how the world appears to her, a mystery about her subjectivity, about what it's like to be a dog, on the inside, as it were.

Sometimes when I notice with what ease Gypsy makes herself at home in the house, or sometimes when she sits next to me at the kitchen table waiting patiently for something to eat, or lies on the rug in my study and gets up to leave with me when she hears me shutting down the computer, it astonishes me that a dog should be part of our family. When we go for a walk and I see people on the

sitting on her mat gazing out to sea

beach with their dogs, I am also sometimes struck by how extraordinary this relation is between human beings and dogs. It is no accident, I think, that cartoonists have found human beings together with their dogs such a good subject.

In part the wonder is that species so different should interact so complexly. My wonder is not about how it came to be that way but *that* it is that way. Marvellous though that interaction is, however, it occurs between many other species. We are delighted when we see it between cats and dogs, birds and crocodiles, and also astonished when we see it between snakes and their prey. I've seen a carpet snake and a mouse become attached to one another when the mouse was introduced after the snake was fed. Rather than eat that mouse, I was told, the snake would die of starvation. Wonderful though that is, the wonder of it does not express what I find mysterious in Gypsy's relation to the family, for that relation is not fully characterised as being between members of different biological species.

Sometimes when I see her on the bedroom or kitchen rug or note the ease with which she wanders through the house, I experience the kind of perceptual flux that occurs when I see now one side and then the other of an ambiguous drawing. In all sorts of ways she is part of the family, participating intelligently and with complex feeling in our lives. But then she does something—chase a cat, for example, her killer instinct aroused—whose nature is so deeply instinctual that she appears wholly animal in a way that invites a capital 'A'. Human beings kill too, of course, and in ways worse than animals do, often coming to savour it, revelling in what Nietzsche called 'a festival of cruelty'. But it is the apparent absence of a psychological dimension in Gypsy's drive to kill that is so disturbing and makes her seem so *other* to us, so much a different kind of being. The occasions for such perceptual shifts—from seeing her as one of us, a member of the family, to seeing her as wholly other in her animal nature—are not always dramatic. The sight of her sniffing another dog's urine could do it. Or the sight of her staring quite vacantly into space, clearly without a thought in her head. Or, as Yael once put it, 'seeing this thing with a tail walking through the house.'

Gypsy Is Old Now

Gypsy is old now. Her beautiful colouring has faded and she is grey. Her eyes are milky, she doesn't see well and she is almost deaf. It is testimony to her spirit that when people see her run in the park some believe that she is a young dog. The truth, though, is that she feels her age in her spirit as well as in her body. This first became apparent to me when we were walking past a house guarded by a young and hopelessly neurotic border collie who barked at everyone and everything. Only a year before, Gypsy gave that irritating crea-ture his just deserts by biting his nose as he thrust it under the front gate. But now she increases her pace as she approaches the gate so that she can get past it as soon as possible. On one occasion the collie's sudden and aggressive bark gave me a fright, even though I was half-expecting it. Gypsy slunk past and gave me a sidelong look which appeared to express humiliation, shame and a question, 'You too?'

I won't swear that her demeanour was in the interrogative voice.

Nor will I press the suggestion that she looked humiliated for that
has obvious, though I suspect not insuperable, difficulties. But I'm
troubled by how to describe her demeanour and how she looked at
me. My problem is not as it would be if I did not know how to
describe a human being's look. If Yael glances at me in a certain
way, is she embarrassed or is she irritated? I may never know. She
may not know. But I ask the question because I know she could
be—she is the kind of being who could be—either.

My problem is not that I am unsure whether Gypsy's demeanour
could be inflected in the interrogative voice. Sometimes it obviously
is; her body quivers with a question. Are we going for a walk? Are
you going to feed me now? Nor do I doubt that sometimes there
exists a common understanding between us or that we sometimes
share pleasures and anxieties. Sometimes, for example, she takes
great pleasure in her awareness that she is sharing something with
one of us. When we are both working, me in my shed with my tools
and she making herself busy with whatever she can get her mouth
around, we have much enjoyment in each other's company, enjoyment that is intensified by the knowledge that it is shared and by
the fact that we are doing something together. She looks at me to
see what I am about to do and, as soon as she has a clue, she tries to
do something in tune with it. My difficulty in knowing how to
describe Gypsy's demeanour when she gave me that look as she
slunk past the gate is that I'm tempted to say that it expressed her
awareness of our common mortality.

Ten, perhaps even five years before, the sudden and aggressive
barking of a dog whom I knew to be safely behind a fence would
not have given me a fright. That it did so when I was in my early

fifties is, I suppose, partly a function of the same biological process that caused Gypsy instinctively to slink past the gate. Though she still has a bearing that evokes admiration in people who pass us on the street and though she still frightens postmen and gasmen, the difference in musculature between her and a powerful young dog is striking. She knows the difference and its consequences should she ignore it. In older human beings that instinctive awareness of increased weakness and vulnerability is transformed by knowledge of mortality. Could it be so in animals?

Often, when I look at Gypsy now, I am pained by the knowledge that she has not much longer to live. For me, the pathos of her condition is increased by the fact that she does not know that she must die. I mean that when she sits beside the table or on her mat in the kitchen or on the rug in my study she does not know that death awaits her. I express myself cautiously here because I fear I may be misunderstood. In his book *The Lives of Animals* J. M. Coetzee gives these words to his main character, Elizabeth Costello—a woman who is driven to the edge of madness by her horror at our incomprehension of the suffering and dishonour that we inflict on animals. She speaks in response to a philosopher who said, as many philosophers do, that animals cannot know that they die and therefore cannot fear death because they do not possess the concepts—of self and of the future, for example—necessary for such knowledge.

Anyone who says that life matters less to animals than it does to us has not held in his hands an animal fighting for its life. The whole of the being of the animal is thrown into that fight, without reserve. When you say that the fight lacks a dimension of intellectual or imaginative horror, I agree. It is not the mode of being of animals to have an intellectual horror: their whole being is in the living flesh.

If I do not convince you, that is because my words, here, lack the power to bring home to you the wholeness, the unabstracted, unintellectual nature, of that animal being. That is why I urge you to read the poets who return the living, electric being to language; and if the poets do not move you, I urge you to walk, flank to flank, beside the beast that is prodded down the chute to his executioner.

You say that death does not matter to an animal because the animal does not understand death. I am reminded of one of the academic philosophers I read in preparing for yesterday's lecture. It was a depressing experience. It awoke in me a quite Swiftian response. If this is the best that human philosophy can offer, I said to myself, I would rather go and live among horses.

It's a fine passage with which I'm deeply in sympathy. Coetzee's words will not, of course, convince the kind of philosopher who is mocked in this passage. Nor should they. The follies of philosophers are easily ridiculed, but, as I've already noted, they sometimes go deep. Only if one has struggled long and hard with the fundamental problems of philosophy will one understand, I think, how easily even the greatest of philosophers can speak nonsense without the slightest awareness that they are doing so. But it is true that the doubts that philosophers express can be so radical that it is difficult to believe that even they could seriously entertain them. Doubts about whether dogs possess a particular concept quickly lead to doubts about whether they possess any. If they don't possess any, then, some philosophers say, they cannot think or even hope that their food is coming because they do not have the concept of food. Anxious to avoid such radical scepticism, other philosophers say dogs do have concepts but they are doggy concepts. Neither radical scepticism nor faith in doggy concepts is a happy position and that fact should incline one to suspect that the trouble may lie in one or more assumptions that both positions share. Perhaps it is the assumption that if a dog is to think or hope or wish that its food is coming, then it must possess concepts.

Coetzee appears to challenge that assumption. He also challenges assumptions about the connection between our sense of an animal's body and of its behaviour and our unhesitating preparedness to say that animals believe this or know that. He urges us to attend to the role that the *living body*, the body of flesh and blood, plays in the constitution of our concepts, including our concepts of belief and knowledge. Like Wittgenstein, he seems to believe that we misunderstand the importance of the infinitely subtle inflexions and demeanours of the body, the many forms of its expressiveness, if we take them only as the basis for hypothetical attributions of states of consciousness to animals. Rather (I take him to suggest), they partly determine the meaning that words like 'knowledge' and 'belief', 'hope' and 'fear' and so on, have in our life with language—language, Coetzee emphasises, as it is used in disciplined ways in literature, and elicited in imaginative living with animals.

Our ways of speaking about knowledge and belief have not been first and fully formed just in our lives with human beings and then applied conjecturally to animals. They have been formed at the same time in our lives with animals. Only some part of that life with animals—and a very artificial part indeed—is the scientific study of them. The philosophical interpretations given to the ways we speak about animals—think of the philosophically emphatic, 'So you think animals have *thoughts*'—are often abstracted from our imaginative living with them and are insufficiently aware of the role played by that living in the actual *formation* of those concepts. I hope I'm not reading too much Wittgenstein into Coetzee. If it seems that way, then take what I have said as merely a philosophical elaboration without exegetical commitment of what I found striking in the passage I quoted. Elaboration isn't a defence, of course, but this elaboration, which exposes unnoticed assumptions, might diminish the inclination to think Coetzee is over the top.

The pathos that informs my sense of Gypsy as a mortal creature who does not know that she will die, does not, I think, conflict with anything I have quoted from Coetzee or with anything I have elaborated in exposition of what I believe to be its philosophical basis. I don't want to say flatly that animals know they die, or to say flatly that they don't. The occasions when I might agree that animals do know they die are confined, I think, to situations of the kind Coetzee describes in the passage I quoted and describes movingly and even more powerfully in his novel *Disgrace*:

> His whole being is gripped by what happens in the theatre. He is convinced the dogs know their time has come. Despite the silence and the painlessness of the procedure, despite the good thoughts that Bev Shaw thinks and that he tries to

think, despite the airtight bags in which they tie the newmade corpses, the dogs in the yard smell what is going on inside. They flatten their ears, they droop their tails, as if they too feel the disgrace of dying; locking their legs, they have to be pulled or pushed or carried over the threshold. On the table some snap wildly left and right, some whine plaintively; none will look straight at the needle in Bev's hand, which they somehow know is going to harm them terribly.

This is knowledge in the shadow of death, and is, moreover, practical knowledge ascribed because of the way the animals behave in the face of danger. My preparedness to concede that dogs may know they are about to die in circumstances such as Coetzee describes or that cats do when, as we say, they go off to die, is a function of the fact that in those circumstances an animal's intelligence is entirely active, its understanding entirely practical. Gypsy believes Yael is coming home when she hears the sound of her car and runs to the back door, but when she lies on her mat she doesn't wonder when Yael will come home, or whether she will be late again. If it is sometimes right to say that she is aware of death, it is never right to say that she wonders when she will die, whether it is inevitable or whether it would it be better or worse to live forever.

Grant, therefore, for the sake of the argument, that Gypsy's look—the look that seems to have asked 'You too?'—expressed not only her awareness of her vulnerability, but also her practical consciousness of death. All that, I think, is consistent with the distinction I drew between the practical awareness and the reflective understanding of death. But I am also tempted to say that Gypsy's look was saturated with her sense of the pathos of our shared mortality. That was how it was with me, when I saw her look and responded to it. Surely, though, it could not have been so with her.

Mortality is a word with profound resonances which speak not only to the fact that we die together with all living things but that, perhaps uniquely amongst living things, we are continuously aware that we must die. Those resonances speak to the fact that we reflect on the inevitability of our dying and on our knowledge of it and hence, of course, on our flight from that knowledge. If death were not problematic for us, if it did not inevitably prompt questions concerning its meaning for our lives, we would never have spoken of our mortality in accents of sorrow and pity and we would barely recognise ourselves.

Because animals have no reflective knowledge of death, they cannot dread it and if they could, they could not take comfort from the fact that they are not alone in their mortality. It is a fact utterly basic to human life that we are consoled by knowledge that others suffer as we do and must die as we must. At first sight that might seem like unsavoury consolation, achieved by taking pleasure in the miseries of others. Really, it is not or, at any rate, mostly it is not. We are creatures who seek to make sense of our lives and the sense we make is never entirely private. What sense we make of our particular lives is always in large part sense we make of the human condition. The need to make sense of death is obviously driven not only by a response to one's own suffering, but also by a more general need to understand what it means to live a human life, and what death shows us about that meaning.

gypsy is old now

Death is so fundamental to our sense of who we are that only when we come seriously to contemplate it do we gain any real understanding of ourselves. Even if someone thinks seriously about death only when they are dying, they must think of death as something that comes to us all, and not merely as affecting us all, but as partly *defining* our human condition. Hannah Arendt has said that the ancient Greeks thought death so important to the definition of humanity that they called human beings The Mortals.

No distinction, I think, is more fundamental in our assessment of ourselves and our lives than the distinction between reality and appearance. Are we really in love or is it love's counterfeit, infatuation? Are we really grieving or are we sentimentally indulging ourselves? Are we facing death bravely and lucidly or have we found false consolation in supernatural hope or in second-rate nature poetry? Do money and status really matter? And so on. These are questions about life's meaning—not necessarily about *the* meaning of life, but about meaning nonetheless. We are creatures who need meaning. Victor Frankl, who invented logo-therapy after his release from a Nazi death camp, wrote repeatedly that his experience as a psychiatrist taught him that people need meaning and that they seek it more desperately than they seek happiness. Some people scoff at that need. They say that those who indulge it are navel-gazing. Most of them scoff only for as long as they are spared affliction.

Sometimes, though, they scoff because they mistakenly believe that the need for meaning is the need to believe that life has an external purpose. It is surprising how many people appear to think that questions to do with the meaning of life should resolve into a question about whether life has an external purpose. Purpose by itself settles nothing about meaning, for some purposes are truly horrible. Wittgenstein put the point more generally when he asked why people think that an after-life should solve the problems of life, or give meaning to life. Why should the meaning of the next life not be as problematic as the meaning of this one? Socrates seemed to have a similar thought when he told the judges who condemned him to death that he hoped to be doing in the next life exactly what he did in this one: putting himself and others to the question concerning how one should live.

But by meaning in life I do not mean even purpose *in* life rather than a purpose *to* life. Indeed, to exaggerate a little, I would say that meaning begins when concern with purpose steps into the background or even ceases. When someone is concerned with the truth about her past but has no particular concern with its usefulness for the future, then she is concerned with the meaning of the past, with its meaning for her life. When someone refuses to live a lie irrespective of the consequences, she is concerned with meaning as I am speaking of it.

Nothing in the very nature of reality requires that we think about such things, but a life that is not answerable to such concerns is barely recognisable to us as fully human. It is hard to imagine someone who really does not care about what betrayal by his lover might show about what their past meant, who does not really care whether their love is real or merely infatuation, who never feels awe and fear and bewilderment in the face of death. There is no metaphysical confusion in thinking that these are questions and concerns that have to do with life's meaning, nor necessarily does concern with them express a hankering for the supernatural.

gypsy is old now

Plato said that we human beings characteristically mistake the necessary for the good. He meant that we are prone to treat as the source of value the things which have become necessary to us because without them our lives would seem meaningless. They are the things to which we give nearly all our energies when death seems distant—money, status, career and so on. Mistaking the necessary for the good is a kind of practical expression of what one believes to be of absolute value—as that in whose light everything else is judged—and it is usually different from what one says really matters. But when affliction strikes, people often reassess what matters. They then imply and sometimes they say directly that we should trust our sense of what matters only if we see it in the light of a lucid sense of our mortality. This kind of lucidity is knowledge in one's heart and in one's bones. No young person would deny they are mortal, yet everyone knows what we mean when we say that they know it only in their heads. For that reason we think that they cannot be wise, for wisdom is possessed only by those who know in their hearts that we are mortal and that at any moment misfortune can deprive us of everything that gives sense to our lives.

Hannah Arendt said that the reason the Greeks thought human beings to be the only mortals is that they believed that only human beings have the kind of individuality that enables them to transcend their characteristics as a species. Animals who cannot transcend their species character have, they thought, a kind of immortality. She is only partly right about the Greeks, I think, but let that pass. The thought she attributes to them is striking and profound. Human beings are individuals in a way that nothing else that we know in nature is.

At least four distinctions can be drawn in the way we mark human individuality. First and least interestingly we are individuals just because we are numerically distinct from other creatures and things. Secondly we are individuals because we have different features and different histories. Thirdly we are individuals because some features that distinguish us from others are striking, making of some of us colourful personalities. This third kind of individuality is sometimes celebrated in political liberalism. More fundamental than any of these, however, is the individuality we express when we say that each human being is unique and irreplaceable, in a sense that can never be conveyed by appealing to individual features, and not just to those who care for them, but unique and irreplaceable period. It does not show itself in the celebration of difference, but in our unfathomable need for particular human beings. The celebration of difference can appeal to reason and to morality or it can offend them. It depends on the differences that are celebrated. But the irreplaceability of human beings in our affections and attachments, without reason or merit, has offended rationalists and moralists since the dawn of thought.

To a degree animals share this kind of individuality with us. They too become attached to each other and to us and some animals mourn for other animals and for us. Because they participate in our lives and lay claim to our loyalty and affection, we bestow on them, in an attenuated way, the kind of individuality which in its full form is unique to human beings. We give them names, for example, though generally they are animal names. (Gypsy is a fine name for a dog, but I always wince when the vet calls her Gypsy Gaita.) And when dogs have no names or lose their names and are given numbers in a lost dogs' home, we don't respond as we do when human beings are denied their names and given numbers instead. It is always to some degree degrading for a human being to be denied his or her name.

The attenuated nature of this kind of individuality in animals shows most clearly perhaps in the fact that we do not write biographies of animals. A character in a story by Isak Dinesen says: 'You ask who he was. I will answer you in a time-honoured manner. I will tell you a story.' That is possible only because the concept of life as it figures in the idea of a story that discloses a distinctive identity—who someone is rather than the sum of their achievements—is what we mean when we say that a person ruined her life, or took a wrong turning in life, or found her life to be worthless, or found in it reason for joy and gratitude. Rush Rhees pointed out that we can say none of this of the lives of animals. We tell stories about animals, as I do in this book, but the stories do not add up to a biography because nothing counts as Orloff or Gypsy or Jack the cockatoo making or failing to make something of their lives, nor even of life making something of them. Life neither presents them with nor denies them opportunities. They cannot rejoice in their life nor can they despair of it.

Isak Dinesen said that 'all sorrows can be borne if you put them into a story or tell a story about them'. A profound observation, I think, but it ignores something very fundamental. We may be consoled by the knowledge that our suffering is shared, but it is also a basic fact that we fear death in a way that is primitive and beyond the reach of the consoling power of stories and poetry. Our primitive fear of death is sometimes thought to be the same fear that we see in animals. Aspects of it are like that; to deny it would be to deny our creatureliness. But an element in it is distinctively human, for it is inextricably bound to the fact that there is something mysterious about the disappearance of the human personality. No natural story about what happens to the body and no supernatural story about the survival of the soul can diminish that mystery and the pain that goes with it.

One cannot understand who one is, the identity that distinguishes us from others, without a sense of what one has in common with others. But equally, in their application to human beings, the concepts that identify what we have in common require us to acknowledge fully that each of us is unique and irreplaceable—unique in a way that nothing else in nature is.

This kind of individuality is not an objective feature of people or animals in the way that individuating characteristics are. Some people are clever, some are silly; some are kind, some are nasty; some are good-natured, some are mean-spirited; some are pessimistic, some are optimistic. While such features may not be objective in the way that differences in height or weight are, they nonetheless give meaning to the claim that we treat people differently from one another *because they are* different from one another. We know what to refer to in order to justify that claim. But if someone were to say that we treat people as unique and irreplaceable *because they are* unique and irreplaceable, what would she refer to? There seems to be nothing.

It is strange and disturbing that something so important to our understanding of human life, and to some degree of animal life, should seem objectively baseless. It is therefore tempting to say that

gypsy is old now

people are irreplaceable only to those who find them so. Have I not emphasised the connection of this kind of individuality with our attachments? The trouble, however, is that we don't mean that. We do mean that all human beings are unique and irreplaceable, period. All sorts of things are irreplaceable to us in a relative sense; these are things that have, as we say, 'sentimental value'—a ring, or a book given to us by a particular person perhaps, or a house or country that has played an important part in our life. But does anyone want to say that people have sentimental value to one another?

Irritation with such talk of individuality prompted Rush Rhees to say: 'If one wants to speak of "individuality", all right. It means little more than "something that can be loved", I think. In any case, one must speak of it in animals no less than in human beings.'

I want to say yes and no to this. Thinking about love gives me more reason to say no. Love is itself answerable to standards which distinguish it from its many false semblances. Love can be pure and it can be base. Rhees himself said there can be no love without the language of love. That language is celebratory, but it is also critical. Indeed it is one only because it is also the other. At the centre of its critical focus is the idea that love must be responsive to the independent reality of the beloved—must be so in order actually to count as real love. That means one must respect her faculty of free consent, that one must try to understand how she sees things, and more besides. But the character of such efforts is conditioned through and through by a response to her as to someone who is unique and irreplaceable. Later, when I discuss a certain form of racist denigration, we shall see that, when people's responses to one another are not conditioned in that way, nothing they do counts as an effort to understand the independent reality of others, to respect their faculty of free consent or to see them as fully another perspective on the world. For the moment, however, I want only to suggest that, were our responses to one another not conditioned by a sense that we are unique and irreplaceable, then love's power to individuate other people would indeed seem like its power to individuate inanimate things—the ones we are attached to for sentimental reasons.

Celebrating an ideal of what he called 'the subjective thinker', the philosopher Søren Kierkegaard spoke of 'the individual' as someone who lived her own life and no one else's. Kierkegaard spoke of her with admiration, knowing how hard it is to be such a person, but he also emphasised that nothing counted as its achievement once and for all. The obligation to 'become an individual' falls, he thought, on each one of us and is a requirement much more important than the obligation, insofar as it exists, to develop our talents. Our very humanity, Kierkegaard thought, was defined by that requirement, and so our humanity was the cost of the failure to rise to it. That might sound harsh or even precious, but consider: for whom does it not matter that they characteristically fall into cliche or banality when they think of important matters? For whom does it not matter that their thoughts are second-hand? For whom does it not matter that what they take to be love is really infatuation, or one of the many unsavoury forms of self-love? Who, when they grieve, does not wish to grieve authentically rather than in self-indulgent ways? Who would not be glad to be complimented as someone others could really talk to, not in the sense of being a sought-after confidant, but in the sense we express when we exclaim, 'At last!

Someone to talk to!' One could go on and if one did one would have identified the various forms of our deep need of lucidity.

The joy of 'finding someone to talk to' is the joy of conversation in which its participants speak as individuals from their experiences, having, as Kierkegaard put it, 'lived their own lives and nobody else's'. Each has something to say in a sense that implies that each has found the voice in which to say it. The pleasure of such conversation is not the pleasure we often find in novelty or in hearing something we had never heard before. It is especially wrong to think of scintillating personalities, bent on distinguishing themselves. One gets more of the hang of it if one thinks of the times when one says that, though one had heard certain words many times before, it was only when so and so spoke them that one sat up and listened and for the first time understood what they meant. Such experiences can be transforming, but the concepts we need to explain why are quite different from those that articulate the pleasure of hearing new theories, or the charm and power of charismatic personalities.

When we find wisdom in words because a particular person has spoken them; when the authority of someone's speech or practical example moves us to take seriously something we had perhaps not taken seriously before, or to find depth where we had not before, then usually over time and sometimes not even very consciously we critically assess whether we were right to believe the words to be wise words, and whether we were right to have been moved as we were. Then we must try to assure ourselves that we did not yield our assent only because we were naive or callow or sentimental or gullible or liable to pathos—and so on. To try to be lucid about these matters is to make our thought answerable to a range of critical concepts that are more extensive than those to which factual thought is answerable, and which are also impersonal in a way that is different from the impersonality of thought about facts. It is the kind of impersonality that is achieved when we have silenced egocentric fantasies because we have submitted to the disciplines with which we rid our thought of banality, of second-hand opinions, of cliche and sentimentality. In what only appears to be a paradox, that kind of un-selfing requires one to become an individual who is truly responsive to the demands of conversation, someone who, as Martin Buber, one of the most famous philosophers of conversation, put it, has become an I to someone's Thou.

Amongst the concepts that mark what we have in common the concept of mortality is preeminent. It conveys more than the mere fact that we will all die. It speaks of that fate in accents of sorrow and pity. It is the uniqueness and preciousness of each human being that gives to our dying the significance, the sorrowful resonance, that the Greeks captured when they called human beings The Mortals. The same accent of sorrow and pity is found in the prayer for the dead in *The Book of Common Prayer*: 'Man that is born of woman hath but a short time to live and is full of misery. He cometh up and is cut down like a flower. He fleeth as it were a shadow and never continueth in one stay.' The necessity to acknowledge both our commonness and also our radical individuality, and the fact that we cannot acknowledge one without the other, creates an irresolvable tension between inconsolable aloneness and the consolation to be found in community. That tension lies at the heart of our mortal identity. The head alone will never really understand it. Understanding is given only when head and heart are inseparably combined. It is not, I think, understanding that can be achieved by anyone afraid of his emotions. Nor by someone whose life has not been touched by sorrow deeply felt and acknowledged.

Clearly, dogs have no such understanding. If they have practical awareness of death, they have no reflective awareness of mortality. The resonances that have accrued to our ways of speaking of mortality show those ways to be saturated with reflection and they come with that concept even when it is used by quite unreflective people. But because of the attenuated individuality that Gypsy shares with some other animals, I have with her a bond that is deepened by my sorrowful recognition that we are both mortal creatures.

The Honour of Corpses

Why did my father lift Orloff over the fence that separated the paddocks from the house and bury him 'at home'? Why did he and I stand weeping at the graveside for some minutes? Why did my father not dump Orloff in a paddock far from the house so that we would not smell his decomposing body? Paddocks in Australia are strewn with the bones of dead sheep.

What we did for Orloff human beings do for each other more elaborately. We did not just put him in a hole and cover him with earth for the many practical reasons there are to do such a thing. We gave him 'a burial', and by standing at the graveside we observed a simple ritual of mourning. But no words were said over his grave, no marker was placed on it and no remembrance candles were lit on the anniversary of his death. That we did as much as we did was an expression of the degree to which Orloff had become 'one of us', part of the family. That we limited it to what we did marked his distance from us, the distance we express when we speak of 'human beings and animals' and when we ask, 'But for a dog?'

Rituals for dead human beings are not only more elaborate than for animals but extend over long periods, sometimes for generations, observed by children and even by grandchildren who visit the grave, tend it, remember the dead in prayers and even, sometimes, light memorial candles thirty or more years after they have died. Perhaps for that reason we accede so easily to the claim, only half true, that such rituals are for us, the living, and were so from the day of the burial.

A full understanding of these things will come only with a psychology that takes seriously the idea of the self, the way it builds up or fragments, that acknowledges the profound role that unconscious motivation can play in our lives, and that has a theory of its interpretation. Such a psychology will reveal the deep ways in which mourning and its rituals are for us. Freud and those who have been influenced by him have had a lot to say on the matter and there also exists a massive and eclectic literature on how we might achieve 'closure', as we now say. I have nothing of detail to say about this, although I may have revealed my sympathies in the outline I gave of what I believe an adequate psychological theory would have to provide. But any explanation we give to the way the rituals of grief are for us will be reductionist if it does not display how they are also for the dead—human and animal. It will avoid reductionism if it shows how rituals for the dead can function for us only insofar as they are done for them—for the dead as irreducible objects of our affections, obligations, sorrows and pity. Freud and most of his followers were at best ambivalent about this.

the honour of corpses

The belief that we should be true to the dead goes deep in the human heart. It is also true that life asserts itself imperiously and with no shame, and we sometimes feel a guilty anxiety that grief for a dead loved one has given way too quickly to life's resurgence in us. Simone Weil writes about this in her *Notebooks* with considerable bitterness:

> There are two lines in the *Iliad* that express with incomparable power the wretched limitation of human love. This is one: 'on the ground they lay, much dearer to the vultures than to their wives.' And this is the other: 'After she was worn out with tears, she began to think of eating.'

Acknowledging this frailty in human beings, some cultures have imposed long and strict conditions of mourning. In the developed West such practices have for the most part been discarded, but were there to be argument about the wisdom of that, the argument would turn on whether those practices were for the sake of the dead or for the sake of the living. For many reasons, the modern temper favours the latter belief. Or, more accurately, a significant part of the modern temper is defined by the fact that it favours it.

When my father died he was buried in a now common service in which the coffin is placed on strips of webbing over the open grave where it sits while final prayers are said. It is then mechanically lowered slowly into the grave. I had known that this is now a common practice but in my grief I had forgotten it. When I saw my father's coffin placed on the webbing, I felt cheated of my last opportunity to help lower him into his grave—'cheated' of the opportunity rather than merely denied it, because it seemed to me, perhaps unfairly, that the practice of lowering the coffin mechanically is yet another of the ways in which our culture encourages us to evade the reality of death. Always with our complicity, of course. I cursed myself for having forgotten the practice, because if I had remembered it, I would have insisted that we who mourned him should lower him into his grave and fill it with earth ourselves, as Jews still do. It may sound strange, but I felt that I owed it to my father to be true to him, and that I could be true to him only if I faced squarely the fact that he was dead.

I speak personally about this. People respond differently to the rituals they think fitting for death, and they think differently about what counts as facing the reality of death. It is therefore easy to see why there are so many psychological theories about how we best come to terms with death and with the complex emotions it stirs in us. But death has always been mysterious, awesome, and fearful to us. Coming to terms with death means coming to terms with *that*. Part of the mystery of death is reflected in the simple surface grammar of the language with which we speak of the dead: we pay our respects to *them*, we erect tombstones for *them*, we bring flowers for *them*, we honour our obligations to *them*, we pity *them* if they are dishonoured and are glad for *them* when things, unfinished in life, finish well in death, when their children are healthy and happy, for example. For some people this surface grammar is an indication either of religious belief in an afterlife or a refusal to accept that the dead are dead and gone for ever. I think this shows a misunderstanding of our attitude towards dead people and dead animals. Why did my father bury Orloff on the right side of the fence? Why did we stand at the graveside and cry? We did it for Orloff.

the honour of corpses

In *Disgrace,* J. M. Coetzee writes movingly about a man who works in a lost dogs' home and tries to protect dogs who have been killed from the dishonour that they suffer when their bodies are disposed of:

The morning after each killing session he drives the loaded kombi...to the incinerator, and there consigns the bodies in their black bags to the flames.

It would be simpler to cart the bags to the incinerator immediately after the session and leave them there for the incinerator crew to dispose of. But that would mean leaving them on the dump with the rest of the weekend's scourings: with waste from the hospital wards, carrion scooped up at the roadside, malodorous refuse from the tannery—a mixture both casual and terrible. He is not prepared to inflict such dishonour upon them.

So on Sunday evenings he brings the bags to the farm in the back of Lucy's kombi, parks them overnight, and on Monday mornings drives them to the hospital grounds. There he himself loads them, one at a time, on to the feeder trolley, cranks the mechanism that hauls the trolley through the steel gate into the flames, pulls the lever to empty it of its contents, and cranks it back, while the workmen whose job this normally is stand by and watch.

On his first Monday he left it to them to do the incinerating. Rigor mortis had stiffened the corpses overnight. The dead legs caught in the bars of the trolley, and when the trolley came back from its trip to the furnace, the dog would as often as not come riding back too, blackened and grinning, smelling of singed fur, its plastic covering burnt away. After a while the workmen began to beat the bags with the backs of their shovels before loading them, to break the rigid limbs. It was then that he intervened and took over the job himself...

Why has he taken on this job? To lighten the burden on Bev Shaw? For that it would be enough to drop off the bags at the dump and drive away. For the sake of the dogs? But the dogs are dead; and what do dogs know of honour and dishonour anyway?

For himself then. For his idea of the world, a world in which men do not use shovels to beat corpses into a more convenient shape for processing.

The dogs are brought to the clinic because they are unwanted: *because we are too menny.* That is where he enters their lives. He may not be their saviour, the one for whom they are not too many, but he is prepared to take care of them once they're unable, utterly unable, to take care of themselves, once even Bev Shaw has washed her hands of them...

He saves the honour of corpses because there is no one else stupid enough to do it.

Puzzled by why he acts as he does, Coetzee's character asks what harm is done to the dog if its dead body is treated brutishly. He answers at first that he acts not for the dogs, but for the sake of a world in which this sort of thing is not done. But it is soon evident to him that the horror of what is done is the horror of what is done *to the dogs* and that the world he hopes for is a world in which

the honour of corpses

dogs are spared the dishonour of having their corpses beaten into 'a more convenient shape for processing'. So he concludes that he acts for the dogs, to take care of them once even Bev Shaw has washed her hands of them, to save 'the honour of corpses'.

People sometimes ask the same question about human beings that Coetzee's character asked about dogs. What harm can befall them now that they are dead? What can dishonour mean to the dead? The dead are dead and beyond all harm, and therefore beyond rational pity, unless, of course, they survive their bodily death in some way. The idea that the dead cannot be harmed is based, I think, on the assumption that, in order to be harmed, a person must at least be capable of being aware of the harm done. But nothing can matter to the dead, so they cannot be harmed.

It is true that nothing can matter to the dead. They cannot be troubled, upset, angry or indignant, their feelings cannot be hurt. But does that mean they cannot be harmed? Is it a truth written in a clear blue sky that if the dead are really dead, if they have not survived in immaterial form to take an interest in what is done to their bodies and their graves and those whom they cared for, that they cannot be harmed? If it is so obvious, why have people through the ages failed to see it?

Priam grieved for Hector whose body was dragged behind Achilles' chariot around the walls of Troy. Antigone grieved for her brother Polynices, whose unburied body was left for the dogs outside the city walls. The colour of their grief was determined by their sorrow and anger over the outrage done in the one case to Hector and in the other to Polynices. When the news broke that Charlie Chaplin's body had been stolen from its grave, people throughout the world pitied him. Could they not let him rest in peace? they asked. Only dull literal-mindedness could make one think that they must all have believed that Chaplin was distressed by what had happened to him. Note how natural it is to say what had happened 'to him', just as it is natural to say of a dead person that we feel sorry for *him* because his grave has been desecrated, or because his children have gone bad, or because he was vilified after his death. Biographies sometimes continue after their subject has died and, depending on how the narrative continues, we may be glad for the dead person or sorrow for him. Does anyone really believe that the post-mortem narrative must be discontinuous with the narrative of the living subject and that it should, perhaps, be marked separately as an epilogue?

If one asks who was harmed, who was defiled when Charlie Chaplin's body was stolen, for Charlie Chaplin is no more, then the answer must be that it is Charlie Chaplin who was harmed. The claim that Charlie Chaplin is no more is just the claim that he is dead and, perhaps, decomposed, returned again to dust and ashes. But does that mean that it was not Charlie Chaplin who was the irreducible object of people's love and pity, that it was not for his sake that a search was conducted, that a new tombstone was built, and fresh flowers brought to the grave? We may, of course, be upset that a dead person's memory is tarnished and be upset for his relatives that it is so, but we are upset in the first instance, surely, because it is bad for the dead person that his memory is tarnished not because his widow is upset. If we sorrow for her, is it not because she sorrows for *him*?

Much the same can be said about our attitude to some animals, with all the qualifications that flow from the fact that their individuality is attenuated in a way that shows in the impossibility of writing biographies about them. They too can be dishonoured by the way their dead bodies are treated. But I acknowledge readily that some people will find that hard to believe even though they accept without hesitation that dead human beings may be harmed. I quoted Coetzee at length in the hope that such people might find him persuasive even if they are not in the end persuaded, and because I want to reflect on what it means to be rightly persuaded by a writer of such grace and power.

Someone who is moved by Coetzee, but who is not persuaded that dogs can be dishonoured by what is done to their dead bodies, would not be persuaded by further facts about dogs of the kind investigated by scientists. It's true that in Coetzee's novel the character who believes that the dogs are dishonoured in death is also the character who believes they know that they are about to die or at least that great harm will befall them, but I do not believe that matters. Nor, I think, will someone be persuaded by reviewing their principles (if they have any) about how dogs should be treated. The question that is at issue now is not how one should treat dogs, or whether one should avoid dishonouring them, but what it can *mean* to dishonour them, especially when they are dead. Had someone said to me, when I was about to hit Tosca over the head with the shovel, 'Don't you see what you are doing!' she would almost certainly have been asking me to appreciate the *meaning* of what I was about to do. And pleading that I should not do it, of course, but pleading because of what it means to do what I was about to do. And if, afterwards, she were to try to explain her understanding of what it meant, she would not tell me about the empirical properties of cats, because she knows there is no dispute between us about that. Nor would she appeal to a principle under which my intended act would have fallen. Or, if she did, it would have to be a principle concerning what it would mean to act as I had intended. But then, if I were convinced by her, it would be because I was convinced by her account of what my act would have meant, rather than because it would have fallen under a principle proscribing such acts.

Why would I have dishonoured Tosca by hitting her on the head with a shovel? That question is in the same conceptual territory as the question, What does it mean to do what my father and I did when we buried Orloff? The question about Orloff does not ask how we *felt* when we buried Orloff: it asks how our feelings were affected by our *understanding* of what we were doing in 'giving him a burial'. It asks whether we have a place in our understanding for the application to dogs of a certain concept—the concept of honouring them when they are dead. Reflecting on that is not a neutral exercise in linguistic or conceptual analysis. It is reflection on how we live our life with this part of language, by which I mean it depends on how the language we use to speak about this might become alive to us, in its creative use, in story or poetry, in theatre or film. Here we often learn, or see sense where we had not before, when we are moved. The person who would try to make me appreciate the meaning of what I intended to do to Tosca might tell me a story, or read me a poem or show me the passage from Coetzee.

The Realm of Meaning

This notion of what it *means* to do something, what does it come to? We appeal often to it. How can you walk past this homeless person who is asking for some change? Don't you know what it *means* to be hungry and humiliated? Or consider the person who, overcome by remorse, says, 'Only now do I fully understand the significance of what I have done.' Sometimes, of course, when we alert someone to the significance of what he has done, we intend in the first instance only to refer to certain consequences. Perhaps an employer was insufficiently attentive to the destitution he brought to a family when he sacked its father. 'You don't fully understand the significance of what you have done,' we might say to him. Usually, however, when we appeal to someone to appreciate the meaning or significance of what they are doing or have done, the facts are visible and not in dispute.

Does that not suggest that what we really intend when we urge someone to an appreciation of the meaning of what he has done is to call upon him to *feel* rightly about the facts, or perhaps to see what moral principles the facts fall under, or a combination of both? The assumption here is that the work of understanding, strictly speaking, is exhausted in the discovery of facts and in subsuming those facts under our principles, or in ordering our principles, or perhaps, in discovering our principles. I am speaking of 'facts' in the workaday sense in which a judge might instruct someone to 'Stick to the facts, please'. It is the idea of the cognitive content that a cool head could extract from an emotive expression or from a fancy literary form.

Understanding—even acceptance—of the facts can, as everyone knows, be distorted by emotion. Hardly any form of human cognitive achievement is invulnerable to distortion by emotion, by desires, fears and fantasies. Even abstract philosophical thinking can be distorted by vanity, by the desire for reputation and by the many other ways in which the fat relentless ego (as Iris Murdoch called it) rules over us.

Since at least the time of Socrates, the West has been preoccupied with the distinction between legitimate and illegitimate persuasion. One version of the distinction—to my mind wrongly attributed to Socrates—says that legitimate persuasion appeals to the head rather than to the heart, to logic and reason rather than to emotion. Suspicion of story-telling and of poetry, as forms of powerful but illegitimate persuasion, often goes with that way of drawing the distinction. Art may delight us, but if it is to teach us, if it is to show us how the world is, then we must extract plain cognitive content from form that often beguiles, dazzles and seduces us.

Another part of the tradition, however, has spoken of the understanding of the heart. To see the reality of another person is a work of love, justice and pity, said Iris Murdoch, placing herself in a long tradition in which love has been understood as a form of understanding. Profoundly aware of how little reality the fat relentless ego can bear, she believed that in becoming alive to the many forms of its flattery, in overcoming sentimentality in art, for example, we allow love, justice and pity to do their *cognitive* work, their work of disclosing reality.

Suppose someone is facing a fatal illness, trying to live the last few months of her life bravely and lucidly. She wants to die well, because for her it is important in itself and also because she feels that the meaning of her past will depend on it. Much of the meaning of what we have done and suffered in the past is a hostage to how we live in the present. The facts of the past are unchangeable, but meaning is seldom fixed. Much of her past had been lived in acknowledgment of the need for us to be lucid if we are to honour our humanity. Were she now to fall into modes of denial or even to seek false consolation, the meaning of her past would come into question. So she seeks knowledge of the facts and asks her physician to tell her the truth without equivocation or euphemism. There is no cure, nothing even to halt the progress for more than a month or two, he tells her and she believes him. She investigates alternative medicines but they offer her no hope, or, to the small extent that they do, hope so slight that to cling to it, she fears, would be to undermine her determination to face and accept death.

For our purposes in trying to understand the forms of persuasion, this is all relatively straightforward. But now a friend tells her that she should not resign herself to death. He quotes Dylan Thomas. He urges her to 'rage against the dying of the light', to express and embrace her anger. She responds that, as far she can see, Thomas's famous words could not have been written by someone who knows the terror of death. Far from expressing dignity, she says, those words express only a fatuous romanticism. She hopes to overcome her terror of death and to accept death, and in accepting it she hopes to find consolation, but she will accept no consolation that is not true to the terror of death.

To resist false consolation is one task, she says. Not to fear consolation because so much of it is false is another, almost as hard and requiring not just courage but also wisdom. She read, she says, *The Last Days of Socrates* and found it powerful and moving, but she could not find her feet with a man who could ask flatly, without qualification, whether death is an evil. How could one ask that and retain a sense of the evil of murder, or sorrow together with those who are bereaved? But in thinking about whether death is always an evil, about whether we should be terrified by it, about whether all consolation is false consolation, she was, she believes, trying to see things as they are rather than as she might wish them to be, making an effort to understand rather than just to control her emotions once the facts were known and faced.

To think rigorously about her imminent death and what it means she must of course be true to the facts. She mustn't fudge them, or let painful ones slip to the back of her mind. She must think rationally, that is logically, to see what follows logically from what, because all efforts at understanding are rendered worthless if one is careless about how one moves from one thought to another. But in addition to all this she must avoid sentimentality and never indulge her disposition to pathos. Always she must resist cliche and that

the realm of meaning

laziness of spirit which, even in her crisis, can make her tone-deaf to it and encourage her to collude with the many ways that words can fail her need for lucidity.

A distinction of the utmost importance must now be observed. It is between sentimentality when it is a *cause* of our failure to see things as they are and when it is a *form* of that failure. When it is a cause it functions as tiredness, drunkenness, haste and fear do when they distort thought and understanding. When it is a form of a failing in thought and understanding then it is a failing in the way that a factual mistake or an invalid inference is a failing. The same distinction applies to our disposition to pathos, to banality and to cliche, to list just some dangers to lucidity when meaning is at issue. The tradition that tells us that we are rightly persuaded only when the head rather than the heart is persuaded, or at any rate when the head is persuaded first and then persuades the heart, always treats those dangers as causes. The tradition that speaks of the understanding of the heart, meaning it seriously to be a form of understanding, takes them sometimes as causes, but always as forms of our failure to understand when that failure occurs in the realm of meaning.

The person we have been considering who is trying to face her imminent death with clarity of mind fell, for a time, under the influence of a charismatic guru who convinced her of the benefits of certain forms of alternative medicine. It was his charisma rather than the scanty, anecdotal evidence he provided that convinced her. He skilfully exploited her vulnerability to sentimental descriptions of those who had the courage and independence of mind to resist the authoritarianism in medical orthodoxy. That is an example of sentimentality distorting her understanding the facts. The remedy would be to get her away from the influence of the guru and to ask her to consider the facts objectively, to consider the scientific evidence, to try to assess what to make of the claims for evidence on the part of the guru's supporters and things of that kind. 'You must let your head rule rather than your heart' would be advice well given in this case.

But consider now her struggle with Dylan Thomas. At first she is attracted to raging against the dying of the light, but later she considers it to be romanticism, to which her sentimentality makes her vulnerable. She believes that raging against death looks like facing death, when really it is an evasion of it. It is not, however, the same kind of evasion as when, for some weeks, she groundlessly believed that the test results that showed positive for cancer were either mistaken or not her results. Thomas's evasion, she believes, is not evasion of the fact of death, but of its meaning. She was tempted by it as she is sometimes tempted by sentimental visions of her reintegration with the whole of nature. Not that all such visions are sentimental. Thoughts about being at one with nature come in many forms. Some are straightforwardly metaphysical thoughts about the survival of the spirit or the ego or the soul. When they are not, they are sometimes expressed in poetry of great beauty and sometimes in poetry of sickening banality.

My father and I did not light candles for Orloff nor build a monument to him, nor mark his grave in any way. Many people do such things, of course. Sometimes when they do it, they are rightly accused of sentimentality—lighting a memorial candle each year for a dead dog would be, for me, an example. A person who lights a candle each year in her home, and has a large tomb built in a cemetery with kitsch statues of the dog, may have false beliefs about the dog, whose falsehood could be specified without reference to her sentimentality. She might believe, for example, that when she spoke to her dog, he always understood her English sentences. She might believe her dog had marvellous powers of telepathy. In response to my remark that no dog can think of philosophy or her sins, she might reply that her dog did both. All this and worse is possible, but none of it is necessary. When sentimentality is a form of the false rather than a cause of error whose nature can be specified without reference to sentimentality (as factual or logical error can be) it need not be the cause of false beliefs, nor be grounded in them.

Our understandings and misunderstandings of meaning are almost always expressed in language in which form and content cannot be separated. When sentimentality is a *cause* of error in, for example, the realm of the factual, then the sentimental expression and the factual content can be separated. Someone might have said to the woman facing death, 'I know it's your sentimentality that causes you to believe in the curative powers of alternative medicines. I can hear it in the way you speak about your guru. But that's irrelevant to whether your claims about those medicines are true or false. Those claims can be investigated by the well-established methods we have to assess factual claims.' But when sentimentality is in the realm of meaning, when it is a *form* of error, that kind of separation of the sentimentality and the truth or falsehood of what the sentimental person has said cannot be effected. When sentimentality is a form of error, it makes no sense to say, 'I know it's sentimental, but that doesn't matter, I just want to know whether it is true or false.' Imagine someone who says, 'I think the Sermon on the Mount is sentimental. But that doesn't matter to me. I don't read the gospels as literature. I read them for their ethical truth.' Would that not be absurd?

What is to overcome sentimentality will therefore be different according to whether it occurs in the realm of meaning on the one hand or in the realm of the factual, the logical or the discursively metaphysical on the other. The realm of meaning in which form cannot be separated from content is essentially rather than accidentally vulnerable to sentimentality. We can dream of overcoming sentimentality, pathos and banality, but we cannot dream of—because it makes no sense to try to conceive of—a realm of meaning in which we are not vulnerable to these failings.

The subject matter of the factual, the purely logical, the discursively metaphysical, the scientific, appears to be accessible to thinkers stripped of any particular form of living. This is a dream of pure thought, of aspiring to see the world as God would see it or, as Thomas Nagel put it in his book *The View from Nowhere*, of seeing the world as from no place within it. Being what we are, human beings of flesh, blood and feeling, we will never achieve such an ideal, but it appears to make sense to posit it as one by which to measure our achievements and define our aspirations in some parts of the life of the mind. And even if we have difficulty in *making sense* of seeing the world as from no place within it, we can make sense of the idea of being free of, for example, tiredness, laziness and vanity. Insofar as we conceive of sentimentality, cliche and so on disabling thought in similar ways, then it makes sense to dream of being free of them too. Perhaps there are thinkers like that somewhere else in the universe.

It is no accident that those who have been inspired by the ideal of seeing the world as from no place within, or as God would see it, have also been chronically suspicious of natural languages, hoping to replace them for all rigorous intellectual purposes with an especially constructed ideal language. Could poets have such an ideal, of escaping the imperfections of English or French or German or Hebrew or Arabic? One need only put the question to know it must be rhetorical. Poets strive to make words live, to fight against the ways language goes dead on us, but they do not strive to create a new language that cannot go dead on us. The life that poetry sustains in language is life that is always threatened by our disposition to sentimentality, to cliche, to banality, to pathos and so on. It is, however, intrinsic to the lucidity we achieve when these are overcome that they are always overcome in the midst of life and never once and for all. It is also intrinsic to that lucidity that its achievement does not find its way into textbooks and encyclopaedias.

Stories, Philosophy and Science

Almost everything that matters in life occurs in the realm of meaning, which is why literature has always been so important to our understanding of life. Without literature—conceived broadly now to mean writing in which style and content cannot be separated, in which a natural language is, as Cora Diamond puts it, 'used at full stretch'—our sense of what we have to think about when we think about life's problems and what they mean would be nothing like what it is and has been throughout our cultural history. Think how often literature and art more generally give us reason to say that we have come to see meaning where we had not before, or deeper meaning than we had thought possible, or even sometimes sense where we had not seen it. These are ways of seeing and understanding that are characteristic of the realm of meaning.

Historically, philosophy and then science have tended to think that to the extent that style and content cannot be separated then the content cannot be cognitive content. It cannot contribute to the great edifice of knowledge. This is half true as I have acknowledged when I said that the fruits of lucidity in the realm of meaning will not find their way into textbooks and encyclopaedias. There is reason to think that the meaning of the word 'knowledge' is largely determined by the prototypes of the kind of cognitive achievements that can be separated from the forms in which they are expressed and which are suitable for inclusion in textbooks and encyclopae-dias. But there is no good reason to think that those prototypes should determine the meaning of all substantial applications of the concepts of understanding, of objectivity, of trying to see things as they are. I grant readily and fully that the understanding of the heart will never lead to knowledge of the kind that can accumulate throughout the ages and become settled in the great encyclopaedias of our culture. But that does not mean that it is not a genuine form of understanding.

When speaking of the understanding of meaning, it is more natural to speak of wisdom or of lucidity than it is to speak of knowledge of the kind that can make one knowledgeable and possibly an expert. How can we determine what is genuinely understanding, or what is genuinely cognitive? Only, I think, by attending to the concepts with which we assess, for different kinds of thinking, whether we are thinking well or badly. If we do this, we will discover, I have suggested, that things we might have assumed to be merely emotive causes of the disablement of cognitive functions turn out really to be forms of falsehood. If that is so, nothing should stand in the way of seeing that in the realm of meaning there is under-standing, different in kind from understanding in the realm of the factual, but not, therefore, understanding in inverted commas only.

stories, philosophy and science

Our understanding of animals and of our relations to them are often shaped by stories. Science and philosophy have commonly assumed that if stories have anything to contribute to understanding of human beings and animals and our relationship to them, then the cognitive content of stories has to be subtracted from the story-telling form and assessed for its factual and conceptual value. This dogma, as I shall call it, of the need to separate genuine cognitive content from literary form, together with the assumption that we are spectators in the world, sure of the contents of our own minds, but only inferentially aware of the contents of the minds of others, has led to reductionism in the study of animals that has sometimes reached lunatic proportions.

The Parrot's Lament is an often charming if sometimes stridently polemical book in which Eugene Linden tells marvellous anecdotes of animals, wild and domesticated. In the past Linden argued with the scientists on their own terms, providing for them (he believed) evidence for a more generous conception than they were inclined to allow of 'animal consciousness'. Now he refuses, he says, to accept the enemy's rules of engagement. He says he will not join arguments he believes to be bereft of common sense—'colloquy out of hell', he calls them. Instead he will tell stories told to him by people who know animals and whose knowledge is not distorted by neurotic fear of anthropomorphism—trainers, zoo keepers and others. Jeffrey Masson, who wrote *When Elephants Weep* in much the same spirit of defiance, said *The Parrot's Lament* was 'an intimate set of animal stories—wonderful, humane, touching. You cannot read it and remain unmoved. This book represents a new way of writing about animals.'

Sadly, for all his laudable determination to write in a different way about animals—the story-telling way—Linden doesn't so much tell stories as pile anecdote upon anecdote, with little care, and with an unrelenting polemic intent. His are not stories to meditate on. Masson is the same. Both men are driven by the need to combat what they take to be foolish scepticism about 'animal consciousness' and yet I detect in them both the desperation one would expect if they knew in their hearts that nothing they can do will lay that scepticism to rest. And that is because, though they start from a belief that the assumptions of behavioural science about objectivity and evidence actually distort our understanding of animal life, they are nonetheless in the grip of those very same assumptions to such a degree that their work remains answerable to the standards of evidence they believe it is wrongheaded to demand.

What is one supposed to do with hundreds of uncorroborated accounts that animals can do this or that extraordinary thing—count, talk, grieve, show remorse? Either one shrugs one's shoulders or one wants more careful description and more systematic and controlled observation, always with one eye on the conceptual questions involved in the description and in the accounts of what more careful, controlled observation might show. One wants, in other words, science in friendship with a scientifically sophisticated philosophy and that is exactly what Linden and Masson seek to escape. Or, more accurately, they do not understand the philosophical pressure to scepticism about consciousness. Not only the basic assumption, but a more general level about, say, the conditions for belief. Both are philosophically naive to an unredeemably damaging degree. But if you stand in the conceptual space where your claims can only be

stories, philosophy and science

taken seriously if they are backed by evidence, rigorously sifted and assessed, then that's the kind of evidence you must provide.

When scientists say they want evidence not anecdote, they do not usually mean that evidence and anecdote are different kinds of things. They mean they are the same kind of thing—empirical reasons for belief—and that anecdotes are an inferior example of it. Even thousands of them cannot add up to what science is prepared to call knowledge.

My sympathies are with Linden and Masson, but something has gone badly wrong. In my judgment it is that Linden and Masson share with those whom they criticise assumptions I have been trying to expose as false. Firstly, they suggest that because we cannot see inside the heads of animals and because animals cannot tell us what is there, our reflective attributions of consciousness to them always depend for justification on the behavioural and other evidence available to us. Secondly, because they treat story-telling as a way of accumulating anecdotal evidence, they assume that the factual is our best prototype for the cognitive. The mischief caused by both assumptions is compounded by the fact that Linden and Masson understand only very imperfectly the difference between a conceptual and an empirical issue. Masson falls into the absurdity of thinking that a spider might have 'a rich inner life and a riot of emotions' because he does not understand the kind of absurdity it is.

With respect to the first assumption concerning the kind of evidence that would justify attributions of states of consciousness to animals, Linden and Masson are right to reject standards imposed on evidence that are not so much scientific as scientistic— that express a quasi-superstitious belief that scientific knowledge is the prototype for all knowledge and that the method that achieves it should be the prototype for all rigorous inquiry.

Crass though it sometimes is, scientism is nonetheless a complex phenomenon. It rests on a variety of assumptions about what counts as objective knowledge and about when doubt can legitimately be put to rest. Some of these assumptions are relatively superficial and are little more than prejudices—that everything should be quantifiable or that in the absence of quantification there can be no real precision, for example. But some assumptions go deep and are deep. Linden and Masson share one of them with virtually everyone who studies animal behavior—namely, that justification for the claims we make about 'animal consciousness' are a function of the kind of evidence we can bring to bear, individually through our experiences and collectively through the generations. Because Linden and Masson hold that assumption they cannot free themselves of the scepticism that follows from it. They therefore pile anecdote upon anecdote, unrelentingly, desperately, with barely a pause for thought or reflection. That is why it is not entirely unfair to think that the only difference between Linden and Masson and those whom they blame for the colloquy out of hell is that Linden and Masson have less stringent standards of evidence.

The second assumption—that factual knowledge is the prototype for all knowledge—prevents Linden and Masson from understanding the proper role of story-telling in their enterprise. They think it is a factual question whether, for example, spiders have consciousness or whether parrots can talk or whether dogs feel remorse. Story-telling, they seem to think, yields factual knowledge that the colloquy from hell cannot because it is in thrall to a scientistic conception of

stories, philosophy and science

evidence and to a conception of objectivity that makes it neurotically fearful of anthropomorphism. Because they think that the cognitive content of their stories is essentially factual, I assume they believe that it would ideally be extractable from the stories, and could be assessed by a science whose methods are not distorted as the methods of science now are. Be that as it may: because Linden and Masson do not properly understand the nature of conceptual questions, they do not understand the distinctive role that story-telling can play in showing us how we can apply to animals concepts we had previously thought had no application to them. Many of our perplexities about animals are not a function of our uncertainty about the evidence, but of our uncertainty about how to describe the evidence and how it bears on our willingness to apply key concepts. Sometimes reflection on those concepts is a neutral exercise of the discursive philosophical intelligence, one that shines in an idiom in which style can be divorced from content. Sometimes it is not. Sometimes reflection on concepts occurs in the realm of meaning. Then story-telling comes into its own.

Here is an example of the neutral kind of conceptual inquiry, hand-in-hand with empirical inquiry. One day a neighbour found Gypsy with the bottom part of a spade—the blade and about eight or ten centimetres of the handle (she had chewed the rest off)—in her mouth. She looked with what appeared to be bewildered frustration at a hole she had started to dig with her paws under the fence in order to visit our neighbour's dogs on the other side.

Was she wondering what to do with the shovel? Was this at least a primitive form of deliberation about means and ends? There is, of course, no doubt that dogs and other animals sometimes use instruments to achieve their purposes, but that does not mean that they deliberate about the use of those instruments or their relative merits—whether this one would do, or whether something better might. Some people would not hesitate to say that Gypsy was deliberating about how to use the shovel. Others would refuse to. It is properly controversial, I think, and disagreement over it would be resolved by careful observation under controlled conditions, observations intended to eliminate this or that possibility, both served by and serving philosophical reflection on what a serious conception of deliberation about means to ends comes to.

A lot of work on animals is of this kind—science partnered by philosophy, each deepening the other. It is obvious why our understanding of animals should be informed by rigorous, controlled observation which is cautious in coming to conclusions. But science needs philosophy if it is not to fall into naivete. Argument about whether signing chimps really are using a language, for example, will not be settled by observation of them, because what counts as language cannot be settled that way. Nor can it be settled by definition. We know, for example, that cows communicate to one another when they moo, but nobody thinks they are speaking or that 'moo' is a word in a cow language. In such a case we see immediately that there is a difference between a sound functioning to a purpose in a system of communication—and it may be a very complex system—and a sound having meaning, of the kind we attribute to a word. What it is for something to be a word has proved to be a very difficult question to answer and there is great controversy over it, not only in philosophy but in the natural sciences where there has been a long argument over whether chimps who have learnt to sign have learnt a language.

I hope, therefore, that readers who might have suspected that my remarks on certainty indicate that I believe that thought about animals is at its best in a science-free zone will cast that suspicion aside. There is, of course, space for speculation, scientific thought and experimentation. But the conceptual space in which that occurs should I think be shaped by three acknowledgments. Firstly, it is not a *conjecture* that dogs have sensations or that they do not meditate on the problems of philosophy. Secondly, that interpretations of empirical observation should be sophisticated concerning the conceptual issues involved in assessing descriptions of what is observed. Thirdly, that while some conceptual questions are best explored in a neutral philosophical inquiry, some are only adequately explored when science and philosophy are friendly with and do not condescend to literature.

Coetzee invites us to extend our concept of dishonour to what we can do to dead dogs. We may accept or reject that invitation and if we accept it we might extend it more generally, or connect it with an understanding of how we can act for the sake of dead animals. If we accept the invitation it will be, I am sure, because of the quality of the writing and the way it has moved us. But if we try to extract from the fact that it has moved us a cognitive content, factual or conceptual, whose character is only contingently vulnerable to the many ways that we are wrongly moved, then we will not have refined our subject matter to make it suitable for, say, science or philosophy. We will have lost our subject matter.

I will leave the last words on this to Rush Rhees. He wrote a letter to someone who had tried to teach him how to discipline his dog, Danny. Rhees failed to discipline Danny, but he says that at the end of his efforts he and Danny knew where they stood with each other. In a way that is inseparable from the fineness of Rhees' prose, we learn, I believe, how to apply to animals the concept of 'knowing where one stands'. One also learns how to apply the concept of respect for a dog's dignity:

> I have never been glad that Danny had the crazy nervous temperament he did have. No more than I've been glad of my stupid impatience with *him*. But…we came to know one another. And what I mean by knowing him—or, if you like, what I mean by *him*—is not something I can separate from being face to face, again and again, with his crazy excitability, with his absolute obstinacy and refusal, with his cussedness in a dozen different ways: trying to meet these, trying to get round them, and generally ending up worse tempered than he and throwing the lead at him so that he ran into the house, and when I got in he was looking at me scared from behind the chair. Scared; but only waiting for the first chance I'd give him to come and press his head between my knees hard enough to break his skull and wag his whole backside.—Gradually, *very* gradually (over a long slog) we came to know one another in all this. He had come to know where he was with me; and I had come to know where I was with him. And each of us knew this.

This comes from a long chapter in Rhees' *Moral Questions* entitled 'Death of a Dog'. It consists of entries in a notebook after Danny had died. Few people, I think, could read the chapter without being unsettled by it, partly because of the pain that is still raw on the page, and partly because of the depth and duration of Rhees' grief. Almost two years after Danny had died, Rhees wrote: 'I do not recover from this loss. When things go wrong over and over again, I am perhaps more constantly aware of this. But it is only a shift in the lighting that may make more articulate what was there the while.—Even the word "recover" jars, for I do not know what I'd imagine in it.'

Rhees grieved for his dog as though for a person. That thought would come naturally to anyone who reads these notebook entries. Natural though the thought is, Rhees makes one wonder what it comes to. He did not think his dog was a person. Normally if we think that someone treats an animal like a person, meaning that as a criticism, then we mean either that she wrongly attributes to the animal capacities that should only be attributed to (human) persons, or that she is mawkish and sentimental, or both. None of this can be said of Rhees.

He feels something like the same bewilderment over his dead dog that we feel over dead human beings. He also feels something like the same guilty anxiety that he will be unfaithful to the dog if his grief abates:

I still do not understand what has happened. I do not understand what it is...

I do not know how to (try to) stay with him and still go ahead with anything.

I do not know what I am trying to do; or: what I am doing.—It is *not*: 'trying to keep the memories vivid'.

But really, for a dog? I do not know what can stop that question. Here is Rhees writing about the kind of presence his dog had in his life:

> When I try to get on with working at (trying to understand) the philosophy of mathematics (mathematical induction, recursion), I realize how, in what I was reading and writing, I made no move without him: how I brought him along in every move. (He was sleeping in the corner or there in front.)
>
> And if he is past—how am I supposed to move?—what do I do here now?

'Poor Living Thing'

On the French side of the Mont Blanc range, rising above the town of Chamonix, there is a beautiful granite obelisk. It is called the Dru. To a mountaineer's eye its granite walls, rising sheer for over a thousand metres until they are sheathed in ice, are one of the finest sights in the European Alps. On one of those walls a route heads with heartstopping audacity directly to the summit. It is the North West Pillar, also called the Bonatti Pillar because Walter Bonatti made the first ascent of it solo.

To climb solo means not only to be deprived of someone who might hold one's fall but also to be deprived of companionship in which one can find comfort and courage. One of the greatest and also one of the most passionate mountaineers, deeply aware of the spiritual dimensions of his calling, Bonatti conceived the idea of climbing the North West Pillar solo during a time of spiritual crisis. A year before he had endured a horrific night at 26,000 feet on K2 in the Himalayas with a sherpa who had become unhinged by the altitude, desperation and exhaustion. Bonatti came close to the same condition. On the eve of his ascent of the Dru he slept in the hut at Mt Envers opposite the Dru, separated from it by the Mere de Glace, but in the late afternoon he took his pack and equipment to the foot of the pillar. For over an hour he sat, brooding whether he had been a fool to conceive of this project that would almost certainly kill him. In his book about this experience, *On the Heights*, Bonatti writes:

> Twilight in those harsh and chill surroundings filled me with a vague sense of awe and for the first time I felt myself a prisoner of the decision I had taken. I envied…all men who did not feel, as I did, the need to confront such trials in order to prove themselves. Filled with these thoughts…I saw a poor butterfly, lured there by the day's warmth, which fell helplessly to the snow a few feet away from me with a last beat of its wings. Poor living thing, what bad luck you had to find yourself about to die in this cruel world, whose existence you never even suspected!…Wretched insect, my brother in misfortune…how much I feel for you and with you. Your tragedy is mine too; what I am searching for in the conquest of the Dru is similar to the intoxication which brought you here…
>
> With such thoughts I could hardly do less than approach it with great tenderness, pick it up and enclose it carefully in my warm hand and take it with me to safety in the hut.

Bonatti's tender pity for the butterfly especially moves me because of the way it is informed by his sense that he shares a common fate with it. True, he expresses that a little melodramatically—'Your

'poor living thing'

tragedy is mine too'—but I find nothing melodramatic or sentimental in his last sentence which expresses his pity with eloquent tenderness. Against the surface logic of the whole passage, perhaps, I tend to read that last sentence back into the earlier parts of the passage and forgive some of its melodrama.

Does Bonatti's pity depend on his attributing conscious states to the butterfly? Does it depend on him believing that the butterfly is afraid when it becomes trapped in the ice? Does he—*must* he—believe it was cold and in pain as it struggled to free itself? I'm sure the power of his pity to move me is not conditional upon my supposing that he believed such things or on my believing them. If someone were to say to me that he found the passage moving but was sceptical of it because its power to move may rest on spurious projections onto the butterfly of responses that occur only in higher animals, then I would think such a person lacked imagination. Not because he failed to imagine the inner states of a butterfly, but because he could not see that he did not need to in order to be moved, and to consent to being moved, by the quality of Bonatti's pity. Nothing in Bonatti's imaginative sense of sharing a common fate with the butterfly requires that he entered with imaginative empathy into its inner life.

The sight of a moth trying to escape the heat of an electric bulb to which it is attracted, but prevented from escaping by the lamp-shade, the desperate frenzy of its struggle, can become painful, even unbearable to some people. So might the sight of a boy slowly plucking the wings off a fly. The latter has become for us a kind of benchmark of cruelty. 'You were probably the kind of little boy who picked the wings off flies,' we say to the sadist. Not, I am sure, because we assume that flies feel intense pain, or any pain at all, but because of the nasty, slow pleasure the boy took in the wanton mutilation of a living thing. To condemn it, one need not even know what to make of the supposition that a fly could be in agony and, *a fortiori*, one need not know what to make of the supposition that the boy took refined pleasure in causing it.

But now I have a confession to make. I quoted only part of the passage from Bonatti's book. Here it is in full.

> Twilight in those harsh and chill surroundings filled me with a vague sense of awe and for the first time I felt myself a prisoner of the decision I had taken. I envied Professor Ceresa who on the next day would get out of this inferno and I also envied all men who did not feel, as I did, the need to confront such trials in order to prove themselves. Filled with these thoughts I was getting ready to return to the hut when I saw a poor butterfly, lured there by the day's warmth, which fell helplessly to the snow a few feet away from me with a last beat of its wings. Poor living thing, what bad luck you had to find yourself about to die in this cruel world, whose existence you never even suspected! In that last beat of its wings I saw before me an almost human drama. Who knows, I thought to myself, with what terror your little eyes watched the last rays of the setting sun, the unexpected metamorphoses of their colours? Who knows with what horror your senses warned you of the fateful bite of the frost, the atrocious certainty of death and, like me, the same infinite regrets? Wretched insect, my brother in misfortune in this place of death, how much I

'poor living thing'

feel for you and with you. Your tragedy is mine too; what I am searching for in the conquest of the Dru is similar to the intoxication which brought you here. The Dru which I was about to challenge was naught else for me than that last ray of sunlight which only a few minutes ago you saw set for ever. If tomorrow I do not succeed in mastering myself, I will share your end.

With such thoughts I could hardly do less than approach it with great tenderness, pick it up and enclose it carefully in my warm hand and take it with me to safety in the hut.

On the face of it, the unedited passage seems unequivocally to contradict what I have just been saying. I said that we had no reason to assume that Bonatti entered imaginatively into the butterfly's state of mind. Yet that seems to be exactly what he did and the logic of the passage seems to suggest that he pitied the butterfly because he did.

That is how it seems, I admit, but I don't believe it is so. The passages which appear to record Bonatti's beliefs about how the butterfly's fate subjectively appeared to it should be read as no more than rhetorical embellishments on a sympathy that did not require such embellishment and which is better expressed without it. I quoted the edited version first hoping to show that the pity for the butterfly expressed so beautifully in it needed no speculative support in order to make it intelligible. It is a tribute to the imaginative quality of his last sentence that its authoritative power could survive the hyperbole that preceded it.

Some people take pleasure in pissing on insects or spiders trapped in urinals. It's a coarse pleasure and betrays a failure of imagination. To piss the spider along the channel of the urinal to the hole leading to the sewer is worse than just casually washing it down the hole, but not because it is worse for the spider. It is a worse thing to do, and I think I would add, a worse thing *to do to the spider*, but not because the spider notices the difference. If one tried to teach one's children not to do this sort of thing or even not to wash spiders down the plughole in the sink, one would be wise to resist the temptation to say, 'Just imagine how the spider feels.' The reason for that is not that the spider must feel terrible in some way or other, but that we could never imagine in what way.

What can one do when someone speculates about how it might feel to the spider except shrug one's shoulders? Ditto to the more radical thought that it must feel some way to the spider but that we will never know what way. Someone might suggest that, on the assumption that being washed down the plughole must feel some way to the spider and that it probably feels bad to it, we should act as though spiders and insects have sensations. Whatever is to be said for that (and that is not much, I think), it should be recognised that one cannot feel tender pity for a creature on the assumption that it is probably appropriate to do so. By far the better conclusion is that speculation about the inner lives of insects plays no part, and should play no part, in the pity we sometimes feel for them.

'Poor living thing.' That is at the heart of Bonatti's response. But life, as I have observed before, is a word with many meanings. Plants are also living things, but they are not living creatures. If a rockfall had pulverised a plant while Bonatti was sitting at the base of the pillar, then, even though he had good reason to fear that he might also be killed, he could not have felt a common mortal fate with the plant, not at any rate one that was informed by the resonances of his 'poor living thing'. His response to the butterfly was informed by the pathos of the weakening beats of its wings, by his sense of its entrapment and by the realisation that the butterfly was attracted to a place that was to prove fatal for it and that would, more than likely, prove fatal for him too. All that enabled him to think of the butterfly as a victim of misfortune. For similar reasons we can think of the spider washed down the plughole as the victim of our thoughtless arrogance.

It would make no sense to speak this way about plants, even though we can care more for some of them—for trees, for example—than we can for any insect. When thousands of trees were uprooted in Britain in the great storm of October 1987, the nation went into mourning. Individuals mourn the loss of partic-ular trees they have known for many years and, I think it is true to say, have sometimes grown to love. Though it may pain one to see a tree disfigured by a lightning strike, or by disease, one cannot I think look upon it as a victim of misfortune. Though one can grow to love a tree but never, I think, an insect, and though the destruc-tion of a tree can affect one profoundly in the way the killing of an insect never could, the sense in which a tree lives and dies is too far removed from the sense in which creatures, including insects, live and die for us to feel for them what Bonatti felt for the butterfly. Bonatti's 'brother in misfortune' is the exaggerated expression of something that we find intelligible, namely that he should feel a sense of common fate with the butterfly. That is made intelligible in its turn because we can describe the butterfly as an actor in a drama that was to consume it. For that reason the word 'killed' has a more substantive application when we speak of a butterfly or spider being killed than when we speak of a tree being killed, even when it is killed dramatically by a lightning strike.

Large cacti grow on the rocky outcrops around Maldon in central Victoria. To my eyes when they are fully grown they look magnificent on the hills amongst the granite boulders, but they have become a scourge in some parts. They spread far and fast and are very hard to eradicate. Driven half mad by them, I imagine, a local farmer took his chainsaw to dozens of them, slashing them to the ground and cutting deep gashes into their large fleshy pads. The result looked grotesque because one could see in it the ferocity of the farmer's attack. One could imagine him on the hillside, wielding his chainsaw with savage, manic energy trying to do what is impossible: to kill plants in ways that only creatures can be killed. I am almost certain that he was encouraged in this illusion by the fact that the dead cacti, their pads discolouring into shades of yellow and orange and stained purple from their exploding fruit, made the barren hillside look like the site of a massacre.

Our sense of insects and spiders as intelligible objects of the kind of pity that Bonatti showed the butterfly appears to depend on our attribution of agency to them, on applying to them, in a substantive way, the distinction between what they do and what merely happens to them. We distinguish, for example, a spider moving to chase prey or to escape a predator from a spider that is moving because it was blown by a powerful gust of wind. We also apply that distinction to robots, it is true, but when we say that a robot's movements are 'purely mechanical', that robots initiate nothing, we imply, I think, that what they 'do' they 'do' in inverted commas.

Some people believe that nothing about the way an insect appears, nothing that we can actually see, can tell us whether it is machine-like in its movements. Only knowledge of whether it has volitions, desires and feelings will tell us that, they say. If it has no inner life, no sensations, no will, then (this thought continues) it does not differ importantly from a mechanical being. That is why theories that explain behaviour, including human behaviour, without reference to inner psychological states, and especially without reference to states that imply will and volition, are called 'mechanistic'.

All this is half true. Were it not for our unhesitating readiness to say that the moth struggles, that the fly wriggles, that the spider tries to escape from the sink, then we could not feel about and respond to them as we do. Nothing less would be adequate to the force of Bonatti's exclamation, 'Poor living thing.' But if someone says that the movements of insects are not caused by inner states of consciousness, that they, as much as machines, do things only in an inverted commas sense, then such a person must be asked where he gets this idea from and why he is so sure of it. Is it written in the heavens? Surely not. Might we not suspect that his confidence rests on the suppressed and unexamined assumption that we speak without hesitation about what insects do, and distinguish what they do from what happens to and in them, because we assume that insects have what it takes psychologically to justify the application of that distinction to them? But that is itself a large assumption about what has given sense to our ways of speaking, one that we have already found wanting in the case of animals.

Bonatti's pity for the butterfly could not have taken the form that it did if he believed it *struggled* against its entrapment on the ice only in a manner of speaking. To see its movements as a struggle is, I think, the achievement of an imaginative capacity, one that is able to see it as a creature caught up in a drama. And that, I suspect, is not so much dependent on as interdependent with our sense that butterflies and spiders are not only living things, but that they also, albeit in a very limited way, have a *life* that we can take an interest in. This is perhaps more true of spiders than butterflies. Over a period of weeks we can watch a spider build its web, rebuild it when someone damages it, chase prey only to become prey itself and flee to the safety of its web with some of its legs missing but getting by with the remainder, and so on. It's an everyday sort of thing, but to see this as drama, even to take an interest in it, requires a certain kind of imagination. To see the drama that consumed the butterfly as Bonatti saw it is to possess that kind of imagination to a high degree.

It is not a speculative imagination, not the imagination that would seek out something hidden inside the insect's head. Everything is on the surface, provided of course one has an imaginatively rich sense of the surface. Recall the words of Coetzee's character in *The Lives of Animals*: 'It is not the mode of being of animals to have an intellectual horror: their whole being is in the living flesh. If I do not convince you, that is because my words, here, lack the power to bring home to you the wholeness, the unabstracted, unintellectual nature, of that animal's being.' The power she wishes that her words possessed is not the power to take one, speculatively, into what is hidden below the animal's skin. It is the power to show that everything that matters is there, that nothing is hidden,

'poor living thing'

that the capacity to see depends on having a rich conception of the surface, a rich conception of what it is to be a living thing and therefore how to describe what it does and what it suffers. 'That is why,' she continues, 'I urge you to read the poets who return the living, electric being to language.' She means the 'living, electric being' of the animals. We could say, 'the living, electric being of insects'.

If our difficulty when we think about spiders is the difficulty of knowing how things subjectively appear to them, then it will seem, irresistibly, to be the difficulty of knowing about something that is hidden from us. Nonetheless, we should resist. Our difficulties are as much if not more about when it makes sense to apply certain concepts. But I want to put that thought carefully. I would not deny—certainly I would not deny flatly—that we might discover that spiders have something that functions like our nervous system does. If we did discover that, then it would be reasonable to say that we now have good grounds for believing that they have sensations. There would—I think most people will concede—be problems establishing why we believe it is a nervous system like ours. We know, after all, that insects are responsive to warmth and cold and to things that cause us pain, but that does not show that their responses are mediated by sensations. If the thing identified as a nervous system merely showed the causal connections between insects coming to the heat of an electric bulb and retreating from it, our scepticism would not be allayed. One could go on in this way, but I won't.

Suppose then that scientific work convinced us that spiders have sensations. There are two inferences that we should not draw. The first is that science has now given us evidence that enables us to say that we know, whereas before we merely assumed, that the distinction between what a creature does and what happens to it applies to spiders, fully, without inverted commas. The second is that the absurdity of believing that spiders have rich inner lives, with reflective capacities, is just the absurdity of believing something that is obviously false. Resisting those (admittedly tempting) inferences is important to defining the right conceptual space in which to locate scientific discoveries about insects.

Sometimes we say that something is absurd, that it is nonsense, because we know that to suppose it is to go against what science has established, or what everyone knew anyway and therefore did not need to be established (that the grass is often green, for example). Sometimes we say something 'cannot be', meaning that the laws of nature make it impossible. If someone were to say that the Earth is flat, or that there are unicorns and mermaids, or that Elvis Presley is alive and well, we would say nonsense. But if someone says that there might actually be mice like Mickey Mouse, mice who speak and fall in love, who squabble with their neighbours and who drive around in little cars, would we mean the same thing when we say nonsense as when we scorned the claim that there are unicorns? And is the thought that stones resent being moved, or that my trousers are relieved when I loosen my belt, nonsense in the way it is nonsense to think that Elvis is still working for the CIA? I think not. While the first set of claims are nonsense, because they go against established facts or against what everyone knows are the laws of nature, the second set go against what one can intelligibly say, what one's words can intelligibly mean, given the life those words have in our language.

'poor living thing'

We have no difficulty in understanding what it would be like for there to be unicorns, or for Elvis to be alive and working for the CIA, but we are mistaken, I think, if we believe we can seriously conceive what it would be like for there to be stones and trousers with psychological lives, or mice like Mickey Mouse. There is, of course, a sense in which we can imagine trousers with an inner life. We could draw a cartoon—the zip as a nose, the crotch as a mouth and so on. We could draw a voice bubble and write anything we want inside it. But what we can imagine in that sense is not the same as what we can seriously conceive. There is nothing which one can seriously suppose it would be like for those propositions to be true. 'Spider with a rich inner life', or 'stone with a rich inner life', are phrases that have no place in sentences which could be true or false or, as I would prefer to put it, no place in serious claims or denials which purport to be claims or denials about the facts. The idea that, though it is extremely unlikely, it might just be true that spiders think about mathematics is like the idea that there might, unlikely though it seems, be mice like Mickey Mouse. Jeffrey Masson's supposition that spiders might have rich inner lives is like that too, which is why I said that its absurdity is not the absurdity of a claim that is obviously false. His failure to see the difference is his failure to see the difference between questions about what one can know and questions about what constrains the application of certain concepts.

Imagination is therefore a complex gift. The great difficulty in philosophy, which depends so much on thought experiments that are often preceded by invitation to imagine something or other, is to distinguish between an imagination that appears to make sense of nonsense by picturing it and imagination that extends our sense of what it is seriously possible to conceive.

Imagination can entertain us and it can also help us to understand the world. Its most creative role in the latter task has often been thought to be the generation of hypotheses that will be brought before a court in which science and a scientifically-minded philosophy sit in judgment. That is one of the important functions of the imagination in helping us to understand how things are in the world. But 'world' is also a word with many meanings. Imagination functions differently when it operates in the world of meaning, and as I have suggested, is answerable to a different set of critical concepts than when it operates in the world of fact. Responding to Bonatti's description, I see how things can be between human beings and insects. Implicit in that realisation are implications for how one can behave towards them. All this is connected with a substantial enough sense of 'seeing insects differently', of 'understanding more deeply what they are'. Imaginative life with language can teach us when concepts can be applied and when they cannot be. Rhees showed us when one can accept 'we knew where we stood with one another'. The authority of Bonatti's pity enlarged our sense of the resonance of 'poor living thing' and of 'my fate is your fate'. Perhaps someone will object that I am saying that poetry can tell how things are. I am. This objection expresses a failure to understand how the critical language works when it works in the realm of meaning and how it is interdependent with a substantial conception of 'how things are', of trying to see things as they are rather than as they often appear to us when we have succumbed to the almost infinite forms of seduction practised by the 'fat relentless ego'.

'poor living thing'

In *Romulus, My Father* I described my father's attitude to other people as one of 'compassionate fatalism'. I did not mean anything metaphysical by that expression. I meant that he thought the human condition was defined by our vulnerability to misfortune. But now, when I think of it, I realise that his demeanour to the whole of life was shaped by something like the same attitude. His demeanour to the animals he raised and cared for was certainly shaped in this way. He took great pleasure in them, but his attitude to them was always coloured by pity for their vulnerability and especially for their vulnerability to human cruelty. His pity extended to all of living nature, to the trees he cared for when they were deformed by disease, and to the countryside when it was parched by drought, the grasses normally golden in summer bleached white and the earth with large cracks in it, some as wide as ten centimetres and as deep as three metres. But it showed in a way to marvel at in his behaviour to his bees.

Bees have always inspired affection in human beings, because they give honey, because they are symbols of industriousness, and because there has been for a long time acknowledgement of their extraordinary 'social' life. Ants inspire a kind of respect because they have some of the same qualities—they are industrious and they too interact in complex ways—but they do not, I think, awaken affection. In our imagination we elaborate on the association of bees with flowers and warm days, and because they die when they sting we readily forgive them the harm they cause us, even though we know they can be deadly when they swarm.

Perhaps that is why my father consented to their stings, never wearing protective clothing when he caught a swarming hive in a nearby tree or when he took the racks from the hives. Though he was never bitten as severely as one would have expected, he suffered enough painful bites for his refusal to don protective clothing to excite concerned curiosity. When I asked him why he refused, he said that he did not think of them as enemies against which he needed to protect himself. I did not fully understand his answer. Nor I suspect did he. But it had to do with, and was certainly of a piece with, his tender compassion for them.

Sometimes on cold mornings he found bees lying on the grass outside the hive, to all appearances quite dead. He would collect them in the palm of his hand and take them into the kitchen where he placed them on the table. Then he would take an electric bulb and move it to and fro, fifteen or so centimetres above them, so they would be warmed by it but not harmed by a concentration of heat on any part of them. When I first saw him do this I was moved by his attentive tenderness and entranced by its results. Gradually signs of life appeared. Legs twitched so slightly that one wondered whether it had really happened, and then more surely so that I knew that the bees had been restored to life by this gentle miracle-worker. Soon they tried to turn right side up, and when they succeeded, often with a little help from us, my father brushed them from the table with the side of an open hand into the cupped palm of the other, as one does breadcrumbs, but gently, and we took them outside where they flew away.

He never told me why they were lying outside the hive. I don't know if he knew or had a theory about it. It occurred to me that they were perhaps driven out of the hive by the other bees and that each morning we collected and brought the same bees to life.

'poor living thing'

Tender though he was to his bees, my father hated flies. If one came into the kitchen, which happened frequently enough, he would not rest until he had killed it. He became quite expert at catching them. He would sneak up on one and, with a sideways sweep of his open hand, palm upwards, catch it and instantly close his fist. People can become obsessive with things that irritate them, even when they are inanimate, like dust or leaves falling in the garden in autumn. But for my father, flies were not just an irritant, even a gross irritant: they were an enemy to be vanquished and he killed them with appropriate satisfaction. Though he was a wise and deeply thoughtful man, I'm sure that it never occurred to him to wonder whether there was some tension between his attitude to his bees and his attitude to flies.

My father's attitude to his bees moved me and transformed my sense of the insect world. Over the years I reflected on it, but not because it alerted me to new facts about bees, nor because it made me wonder whether the facts I knew required me to bring my conduct towards insects under principles I had hitherto applied only to my conduct towards animals. He taught me what compassion for an insect could be and what behaviour to them could mean. He taught me by his example, but I do not think of his example as having introduced me to something I could assess independently of the authority with which it moved me.

At about the same age she was when she told me, so assuredly, that one cannot have a pain in one's pocket, my daughter Katie and I were watching a nature program on television. We saw baby rodents, more ugly even than baby rats, under the desert sand of Saudi Arabia. 'Look at that,' I said to Katie. 'Aren't they awful.' With little hesitation, she replied that they were also God's creatures.

I was humbled by her response, ashamed, in fact, that such simple words should show up the grossness of my attitude. I could think of no words that could express better and at the same time so simply this wonderful acceptance of all living creatures. Later, when she fell under the influence of different teachers, she would say, 'Poor nature,' whenever she inadvertently stepped on a snail or some other small creature and even when she accidentally crushed flowers under her feet. I thought this relatively shallow pantheism, modulated by a fashionable environmentalism, a poor exchange for how she had previously looked at the natural world.

Had I taken her earlier remark that those rodents, ugly as they were, are also God's creatures, as expressing a claim that rested on metaphysical speculation about the causes of life—speculation of a kind that is thought to be in competition with naturalistic explanations of the universe—I would not have found it impressive. I would have said that, though some people believe this, I did not. As it was, her words silenced me completely. True, I didn't say yes, they are God's creatures, and had she asked me whether I believed in God then I would not have been able to say that I did. I put it that way, that I would not have been able to say that I did, rather than more simply that I didn't or that I was an agnostic, because I don't think I understand what it means, to believe in God, what kind of believing it is to believe in Him.

My admission that I don't think that I understand what it means to believe in God will irritate some people, I know, because they will associate it with attempts to hold on to the emotional benefits of religion while refusing to accept the intellectual responsibilities of belief. Religious propositions are clear enough in their meaning, they will say. The only serious question is whether they are true. To suggest otherwise is to encourage obscurantism. This is an old disagreement. It is between those who believe in the God of the philosophers and those who proclaim the God of religion.

The God of the philosophers is a metaphysical entity whose properties, if not His existence, are given to reason of the kind I described earlier—reason idealised as operating perfectly when it is free of the disturbances of practical and affective human living. The God of religion, on the other hand, is defined by the requirement that belief in Him must deepen our ordinary human understanding of what matters in life. No one can seriously say, 'It is cheap, sentimental, banal and does the dirt on life, but it is my religion and true nonetheless.' Religious claims are always made fully in the realm of meaning. Metaphysical claims about the God of the philosophers, on the other hand, are most clear-sightedly made when one sees the world as from no place within it. Or so their proponents believe. The God of religion knows our sins, our joys, our woes, and all that is in our hearts. The omniscient God of the philosophers knows all that and also our email addresses. Those who believe in such a God are undeterred by the banality of that understanding of what it means to say that God knows everything. But for those whose God is the God of religion it represents a misunderstanding of the grammar of how people seriously speak of an all-knowing God in their religious lives, in prayer and in worship.

Katie's words silenced me because they resonated against a part of our religious tradition in which to speak of the world as God's creation is, at one and the same time, to speak of it with gratitude as a good world given to us as a gift. In that tradition one did not first believe in God and then as a further step, perhaps of inference or perhaps of faith, believe that the world as He created it is a good world. Belief in God as the creator of heaven and earth is inseparable from gratitude for the world He has given us. Disillusionment with the latter is the diminishment of faith in the former. To say that one knows there is a God, but that one is not sure whether the world He created is deserving of our unconditional love, is as strange, in this tradition, as saying that one knows there is a God but that one is not sure whether he created the world. Katie's words silenced and shamed me because I took them as expressing the deep truths of that tradition, and that is also why her later pantheistic expression of condolences to nature looked shallow by comparison.

Although the unconditional love of the world has, perhaps, been expressed most finely and most simply in parts of our religious tradition, such love does not depend on explicit religious belief or metaphysical commitment. In *The Myth of Sisyphus* Albert Camus expressed it, not only withholding such commitments but defiantly rejecting them and he did so implicitly, but more beautifully and with no philosophical pretensions, in his lyrical essays on Algerian cities and landscapes. Pablo Casals also expressed it in his autobiography.

For the past 80 years I have started each day in the same manner. It is not a mechanical routine but something essential

'poor living thing'

to my daily life. I go to the piano and I play two preludes and fugues of Bach. I cannot think of doing otherwise. It is a sort of benediction on the house. But that is not its only meaning for me. It is a re-discovery of the world of which I have the joy of being a part. It fills me with awareness of the wonder of life, with a feeling of the incredible marvel of being a human being...

I do not think a day has passed in my life in which I have failed to look with fresh amazement at the miracle of nature.

Because I have quoted this in more than one place I apologise to anyone who has read me quoting it before, but I know of nothing that expresses so poignantly, so briefly and, to my mind, so convincingly an unconditional love of the world without religious commitment. Casals says that he thinks that not a day has passed 'in which [he has] failed to look with fresh amazement at the miracle of nature'. I do not think that he means merely that he has been lucky to experience every day for eighty years what most of us experience only occasionally when we wake up to a fine spring morning and are glad to be alive. To wake up feeling like that is of course a joy, and to do it for even half the days of one's life would be wonderful. But that experience repeated every day for eighty years would be just that—the contingent repetition of something that might have occurred only once. It could not, of itself, yield a perspective on the world from which suicide could appear, as it did to Camus, as a species of ingratitude, nor could it of itself yield a perspective from which the quest for lucidity could seem like an expression of gratitude for a life valued as a gift.

Casals does not speak explicitly of life as a gift, but he does not need to: the entire passage is written in the key of gratitude. If someone were now to ask whether one could lucidly respond to life as a gift without asking who gave the gift, then I would say that the passage from Casals shows that one can. I would go further. To someone who says that there is intellectual dishonesty in speaking of life as a gift unless one answers whose gift it is, I would answer that if this literal-minded thought is to be rescued from banality then talk of life as God's gift must be infused with the same love of the world that Casals expressed. But can one achieve that merely by consenting to a series of metaphysical propositions? And if metaphysics cannot take one there, then what need has one of it?

Imagine this: one believes in a first cause, creator of the world whom one calls God; then one believes that He gave us life and sustains it in us; then that He gave life to us as a gift; then that it is a gift deserving of our gratitude; then that it is deserving of our unconditional gratitude. Others might want to put in more or fewer steps, but the point, I hope, is clear even if still controversial. Such a long series of inferences cannot take one to the place where Casals was able to express his love for the beauty of the world and his gratitude for a life that appeared to him a gift.

Simone Weil, who wrote as finely of the love of the beauty of the world as anyone I know, called this love a form of the implicit love of God. It cannot be denied that there is a gulf between those who can speak God's name in prayer and in worship, those who can say, with all their heart, that the world is God's creation and that He loves all its creatures, and those who cannot. But to say with all one's heart that all creatures without exception are God's creatures is not just

'poor living thing'

sincerely to assert a metaphysical proposition about the causal origins of life on earth.

When Katie gently rebuked me, it was not the awesome metaphysical edifice that theologians and philosophers have constructed when they elaborated the God of the philosophers that silenced me, impressive though that is. It was the heartrending beauty of some of the expressions of the love of the world and its creatures that her words brought to mind. Casals' hymn of gratitude for life is amongst them. It is impossible to imagine him rising from the piano and casually crushing some insects or plucking the wings off flies. Can we imagine him catching flies in his hand and killing them with sweet satisfaction? About that, I have no opinion.

Sacred Places

Katie's 'Poor nature'—a generalised and not entirely authentic concern for nature in general—was a sad decline from her affirmation that all animals without exception are God's creatures. It had the one advantage, however, of integrating a concern with animals with a concern with the natural world more generally—with living things like grasses, flowers and trees that are not creatures and also with inanimate nature. Almost thirty years before I began to write this book I thought of writing about human beings and their relation to nature by way of writing about my experiences in the mountains. Now, after so many years, I will do it in this chapter. It would be a strange bond with animals, I think, that was not at the same time an expression of a love of nature.

We were all exhausted. None of us, I think, had carried a pack before. I hadn't walked further than the corner shop since getting my driving licence five years earlier. Now we needed to rest after carrying packs of around thirty kilos for three days up and down steep tracks high in New Zealand's mountainous and densely forested Fiordland. We were there because a New Zealand friend had convinced me to go tramping, as they call it in New Zealand. While my companions were resting in the hut, I went alone for a short walk towards the ridge that defines one side of the Hollyford Valley. It was raining, but the wind was high and clouds swirled dramatically, parting every so often to reveal blue sky, encouraging my hope that when I reached the ridge I might be able to see across the valley—but when I got there, I could see nothing. Disappointed, I turned to return to the hut, but had taken only a few steps when something prompted me to turn around. Through a break in the clouds, across the valley, I saw a mountain of dramatic nobility, trailing a snow plume. Her name was Mount Christina. Moved almost to tears by her beauty, I resolved I would become a mountaineer.

As soon as I returned to Australia I bought a climbing instruction book (the famous Blackshaw), boots, a rope, karabiners and slings, and with some anxious friends went in search of cliffs to climb. I recall vividly the first time when, on a beautiful early summer's morning, the same friend from New Zealand and I stood at the base of a cliff some eighty metres high in remote and dense Australian bushland, and with our hearts in our mouths tied on to the rope. As I laid my hands on the cliff face I experienced a sensation that I was to savour in years to come—the sensual feel of hands on warm rock, fingers tracing its contours to find a safe hold. I climbed the first ten metres or so and knew that we were committed. Pride alone would ensure that we would get to the top or fall.

sacred places

Just as vividly I recall the comic scene that occurred only a month or so later when I was standing on a small ledge, some eighty metres above the ground, on a sheer and sometimes overhanging face. It was again a beautiful summer's day and I was enjoying the shade of an overhang as I surveyed the golden wheat fields of the Wimmera. I had tied myself to the rock face and was belaying my friend from New Zealand. From the amount of rope I had paid out I estimated that he was six or seven metres above me, but the over-hang prevented me from seeing or hearing him. It seemed to me that it had been a long time since he had started the pitch, but though it was the first time he had led, the day was so glorious, the scenery so entrancing, and the adventure so exhilarating, that anxious thoughts had no room in my mind.

I think I had just started whistling a tune when a flake of rock fell past me. I hardly saw it disappear when I saw my friend plum-meting silently behind it—because, he told me later, he was too terrified even to scream. Climbing the overhang had drained the strength from his arms, which began to feel like wooden blocks and he peeled off backwards, dislodging the flake as he did so. When I saw him flying past I was too shocked to do anything but hold the rope tight. I don't know how much rope slid through my gloved hands, but when it stopped, and I realised that he and I were still tied to each end of it and still high on the face rather than at the bottom of it, I whooped so loudly and repeatedly with pleasure that I must have been heard for miles across the wheat fields, perhaps all the way to Natimuk. Everything—the bowline knots which tied us to the rope, the figure-of-eight knot which anchored me to my belay, the chocks we placed in the crack to secure the belay—worked just as Blackshaw said it would if we did it properly. I could hardly believe it. The cost was merely a bone chipped in my friend's ankle as he crashed back into the face when I stopped his fall.

We were accused of being irresponsible, climbing like that without first serving an apprenticeship with experienced climbers. Perhaps we were, but climbing clubs were uncongenial to our anarchistic temperaments. And instinctively we knew that to face the challenge by ourselves, with only Blackshaw and the great climbers we had read about as companions, would yield to us an adventure of a kind and intensity we would surely miss if we had the comfort of someone experienced beside us. We would not have missed the adventure for the world.

Even so, I have often reflected on the accusation that we were irresponsible. I have never taken it seriously when it comes from the kind of person who would weigh down young climbers with so many spare socks and emergency supplies that they are bound to be caught out after dark because their packs are too heavy. Nor by those— often the same people—who would wish the mountains always to have the appearance of danger but never the reality. Mountaineering is degraded unless the prospect of death is lucidly accepted. To discover after one has come close to death oneself or after a climbing partner has died that one climbed only because one never really believed that one would be killed is a demeaning experience for anyone who has climbed for any length of time. This is because, for most mountaineers the risk of being killed is integral to the experience that attracts them to the mountains. If we were immortal, mountaineering would not exist or only in a form unrecognisable to us. The risk that one might be killed is inseparable from the intensity of the joy that mountaineers sometimes experience and crave to experience again. It is a joy they cherish, but only insofar as they believe they really are prepared to die. If they should discover that it was an illusion, that in their hearts they never believed they would die, then those intense experiences would become worthless.

One can, of course, have experiences whose intensity depends on the risk of death soloing on a six-metre boulder or sky diving or driving a racing car. For most mountaineers however the intense joy is joy in the beauty of the mountains which they experience as a gift granted to them only because they have risked their life for it. This is romanticism, of course, with all that is suspect in it, but it is romanticism tempered by the disciplines of skill and concentration necessary to stay alive for more than a season in the high mountains.

Vulnerable to that romanticism, I never yielded entirely to it because for all the years that I climbed I was conscious of how deeply it upset my father. He never properly understood the reasons why I climbed and insofar as he did he scorned them. He would climb mountains too, he said, if it were necessary to secure food or seek medical help for his family, or for any other necessity presenting itself under the guise of duty. His attitude was one that dominated the European poor for whom necessity—especially the necessity to provide for one's family—could redeem and give dignity to a life whose crushing burdens would otherwise drive one to despair.

Of itself, that attitude was enough to make it offensive to him that I should choose to do what no sane person would do unless they had to. More deeply even than that, however, he was offended—sometimes I think he found it obscene—that I could (as he saw it) hold my life so cheap. Certain experiences in his life had brought him to look upon suicide as something terrible even when it caused no harm to anyone else or showed no obvious vice, such as cowardice in dealing with one's problems. I doubt that he would have thought it morally terrible. Schopenhauer caught something important in the attitude to suicide of people like my father when he said that the problem of suicide is too deep for morality.

My father believed the death of mountaineers to be terrible in much the same way as the death of someone who had committed suicide. The virtues of character that I praised in the great mountaineers were for him false virtues. In circumstances of genuine necessity, he said, the courage shown by mountaineers would be a virtue, but exercised in the reckless lack of regard for one's life and for one's responsibilities to others it was a counterfeit virtue. In this he reminded me of a philosopher who had commented on the ancient doctrine, to be found in Plato, Aristotle and later in Aquinas, that the virtues formed a unity, that one could not possess one unless one possessed at least many of the others. The philosopher argued that a person who risked his life for an evil cause might show courage, but courage was not a virtue in that person. My father's anger at my mountaineering exploits was in part fuelled by his fear for my safety, but it was also informed by the belief that it went against everything that had deepened his life and for which he was grateful.

Many mountaineers do of course bring what they do under various concepts of necessity. They say that they must climb, that they cannot give it up. Bonatti says in the passage I quoted earlier that he curses the need to prove himself, wishing he were free of it as most people are. For him, the need was not to prove himself to others, but to prove to himself that he possessed certain virtues even in the face of death—not death in the mountains but in the face of death period.

Most people live their lives without worrying about whether they would have the courage to face death. For others it can be very important to know what they would do if they were sitting on the train next to a person whose safety was threatened by a gang of thugs. Would they intervene, or would they sit quietly hoping to be left alone? What would they do, they ask themselves, if they lived in a country in which a neighbour might disappear in the middle of the night at the hands of the secret police? Physical courage has been devalued in most western democracies where people are lucky that moral courage seldom needs physical courage to support it. Most of the peoples of the earth are not so lucky.

It is not therefore because they are morbid that men like Bonatti are tortured by doubts about their courage. In the mountains they seek to know not what kind of mountaineer they are, but what kind of human being. That is why it is so shaming to know that one has proved a coward even when no one has suffered the consequences of one's cowardice. But the knowledge that cowardice led one to abandon one's partner is devastating. Friendships developed in the mountains between the most unlikely people may be sustained for a lifetime because each knew they could rely on the other's courage. And, of course, close friendships have been broken when one climber proved a coward. But though it is devastating to learn that one is a coward, to have been brave in the mountains is not a good reason for believing that one will be brave elsewhere. It is one thing to risk death, to face it courageously in a blizzard or when someone has fallen, and another thing to face it in the guise of a slowly degenerative illness, and another thing again to have the courage to remain human in a concentration camp.

Most mountaineers do not, I think, treat the mountain as merely a preferred environment in which to learn about themselves what racing-car drivers learn just as well. Most mountaineers (though perhaps not all rock climbers) love to be in the mountains and, though they may much prefer the mountains over the low country or even over the sea, their love of the mountains is an expression of their love of nature. Their love of nature shows itself in their love of the mountains just as a love of humanity can show itself in the way one loves one's friends, or a love of womanhood in the faithful love of one's wife. Their love of nature does not just add a further reason why they need to climb—it generally transforms that need. The self-knowledge they are compelled to seek is no longer just whether they have this or that virtue or failing. They seek to understand themselves through an understanding of the human condition and in the mountains they seek an understanding of that in its essential relation to nature.

Writing in a climbing journal in response to acrimonious arguments about climbing ethics—about when one may use a piton or a bolt, or when, in the Himalayas, one may use a ladder and so on—a distinguished British mountaineer pointed out that if one were to judge by the passions the argument aroused, one might be misled into thinking that it was not about climbing ethics, but about 'real ethics', by which he meant about morality, about rules (as he put it) that govern our relations to people rather than to cliffs and mountains.

sacred places

Mountaineering literature is, of course, filled with heroic and noble stories of people sacrificing themselves for others, but debates about 'mountaineering ethics' are usually about the relatively artificial constraints that are now imposed on how one can legitimately get up a mountain or a rock face.

Though rock climbing may become an Olympic sport, the big arguments in mountaineering have not been about standards that might govern mountaineering practice as the rules of a sport govern the players. That is because all sports are artefacts, as it were, created by their rules and the rules can be made and modified by a committee. I do not mean to trivialise sport by saying that. Concern with character is fundamental to most sports. Our interest in them is hardly ever just an interest in how a human machine can perform, but how a human being can overcome weariness, demoralisation, temptations to be a bad loser or even to cheat. Were this not so sport would be of no interest. But no sportsperson, I think, can say in his defence, when he has broken the rules of the game, that his conscience required him to play as he did.

Mountaineers may be competitive and vain to an astonishing degree, but reflection about how one may legitimately climb a mountain is not intended to enhance the competitive dimensions of the practice. It is to alert the climbing fraternity about how advances in climbing techniques and in the technology of climbing equipment can threaten the respect for the mountain, a respect that at its best is deepened by a love of its beauty. That, rather than the fact that mountaineers tend to be an anarchistic lot, is the reason why disputes in mountaineering ethics can never be settled by a committee. Like morality, mountaineering ethics looks to be a matter of discovery rather than decision, and to some degree always a matter of conscience.

When a fine mountaineer climbed a peak in the Andes with a pneumatic hammer with which he inserted bolts and, I think, aluminium ladders, there was widespread anger that he had made it easy for himself. Deeper, though, was the outrage that he violated the mountain and betrayed the love of nature that should be at the heart of mountaineering.

The writer who distinguished between real ethics and mountaineering ethics was more wrong than right. It is an old ruse of morality to make it seem that only moral value can go deep with a morally serious person, and that such a person could never, except through confusion or self-deception, think that any other value could compete with moral value. The ruse has been remarkably successful. Because the need to climb is sometimes so transparently in conflict with family obligations—death may deprive a family of a parent—it is sometimes turned into a moral need in order to make it look more respectable when it conflicts with other moral obligations. Thus the mountaineer who is torn between his need to climb and the responsibilities to his family begins to look like someone who is merely torn between conflicting moral obligations. Either that or he is plainly irresponsible or in the grip of pathological needs.

It is, I think, a moralistic conception of morality that would claim for itself all serious value that conflicts with it. We should resist its imperious claims. The need to climb can go deep and when it does its depth is not merely psychological. For though it may be true that the climber's need is in part a need to be true to himself, the values in whose light he understands what it is to be true to himself are not reducible to a value-neutral psychology. Sometimes—at the best times—the necessities of mountaineering, the reasons why climbers must climb, are like moral necessities, outward-looking, and also like moral necessities they are distorted when one tries to explain them by an inward-looking psychology.

Like other values the deepest values in mountaineering can show themselves in what seem to be trivial details. Even when the need to climb is justifiably called a spiritual need, in which other needs for, say, self-knowledge are transformed by an almost mystical love of the beauty of the world realised in the mountains, that need can show itself in one's attitude to the use of pitons or bolts, or even in how one climbs. Shame that one allowed oneself because, for example, one is unfit or because one lacks the climbing skill, to be dragged up the face, second on the rope, like a sack of potatoes, can go well beyond personal pride. It can be an expression of respect for the mountain. No one who climbs a mountain because of its beauty could climb it like that. Climbing it properly, with some grace and without excessive use of aids, can be an expression of love for the mountain, rather than an expression of the need always to perfect one's standards, to climb harder, more elegantly as an ideal in itself.

Many mountaineers speak of their relation to the mountains in words more normally used in speaking of relations to persons— they speak of respect for the mountain, of gratitude that though they were reckless in their climbing, the mountain had let them off lightly. Sometimes they speak obsessively of it as a foe to be vanquished. But of course, no mountaineer believes that mountains are persons. Mountaineers speak in metaphors that enable them, sometimes in powerful ways, to express the fact that their will is limited by necessities that are nothing like the rules of a game and seem like nothing that a group could impose, and that they are driven by necessities whose nature is to be explained by things external to themselves.

If is of course true that one cannot rationally feel guilty towards a mountain. No one rationally feels remorse for placing more pitons than he should have. Mountains cannot be wronged. And if someone feels ashamed for making an ascent with unnecessary aids, then he is not ashamed in front of the mountain. But this should not lead to the conclusion that the outward-looking references are illusory, that the shame is self-regarding, a function of the standards of achievement and of character that one has set oneself.

A different kind of example might help to clarify what I mean. I remember an occasion walking with my father's friend Hora when he stopped, the expression on his face transformed by wonder. 'Look,' he said, 'how amazing life is.' He was pointing to a blade of grass that had reached to the sunlight through a small crack in the concrete. He knew, of course, that there was a perfectly natural explanation of why this blade of grass had managed to grow there, an explanation that anyone could accept without responding as he did. And that same explanation would reveal that, considered only as an event, this was not one to wonder at. Hora knew all that. He wasn't expressing puzzlement or even astonishment. He was expressing his reverence for nature, a reverence that always existed in him, but which the sight of that blade of grass had brought again to a pitch of intensity.

Suppose now that someone had been with us and that, when he heard Hora's exclamation of wonder, he crushed the blade of grass with his foot—perhaps because he was angry with Hora—scraping his foot up and down over it until nothing was left, just a green smear on the concrete. There is more than one reason why this person might later be ashamed of himself. He might be ashamed for the way his action was directed against Hora whom he knew to be a good man. He might be ashamed because of the pettiness and coarseness that his actions revealed. But, in addition to this, he might feel humbled by Hora's reverence for life and come to see in what he did not just the expression of petty and base motives, or an offence against Hora, but an offence against the life that Hora revered. Hora could not have done what the other person did and an account of that impossibility should not look to Hora but to the world his wonder revealed.

So it might become for the person who crushed the blade of grass. And so it sometimes is for the mountaineer who cannot continue a climb when he knows he could do so only by driving in bolts. To understand why he cannot, one should look not to his psychology, but to an understanding of how it can see this as a defilement. Love is everywhere distinguished from its false semblances by the way in which one respects the independent reality of what one loves. This is obvious in the case of human beings, but it is also true of animals and nature.

So much talk of the love of nature may seem an example of the romanticism I had earlier claimed to keep at a distance. The great tradition of mountain romanticism focuses on the European Alps. Grand, noble and savage though they may be, when one climbs in the Alps one is never far from civilisation. Only half an hour or so before one reaches a barren landscape of rock and ice, one was walking through a summer field. Descending from the bleak world of the glaciers and peaks, lifeless and intimidating, the roar of crashing stones and avalanches still in one's ears, it is hard to describe the joy of lying in the high, soft, green meadow grass, amongst the wild flowers, listening to the bells around the necks of the goats and cows and dozing for perhaps an hour before going down to the village. For a time after the intensity of the glories and the miseries of an Alpine ascent, the return to the village is unsettling, even alienating, but a large tub of French ice-cream followed by a steak with salad and olives, on a sidewalk café surrounded by ordinary people, gradually restores one to the human world and an ambivalent acceptance of its everydayness. In every Alpine village one sees young men and women whose faces radiate the joys of their adventures or, sometimes, betray the terrors of avalanches and lightning in the high mountains or the bitter exhaustion of their efforts to accept that their climbing partner is dead. Nowhere else in the world, I think, can one experience such dramatic contrasts as in the European Alps. They have nourished romanticism in generations of mountaineers.

In Australia it can be different. Though the mountains are not dramatic they are remote and their flanks are covered in often impenetrable scrub. In the winter of 1971, well before eco-tourism and even before the widespread popularity of ski touring, I went with three friends to the Cradle Mountain National Park in Tasmania. We went looking for ice-climbing in the gullies that cut the vertical precipices of Mt Geryon. As far as I know we had the entire park to ourselves. Certainly we saw no one in the two weeks we were in it. As well as heavy climbing equipment and clothes we had to carry enough food to last the fortnight. Our packs weighed just under forty kilograms. When we fell over, as we often did, stumbling over the slippery roots of beech trees, or over the infuriating button grass, we could not get up without help.

We left the end of Lake St Clair later than we should have and dark caught us as we emerged from the forest, with less than a kilometre to go to the hut. In the dark we lost the path and found ourselves wading, sometimes waist-deep, in a swamp, frustrated that we were close to the hut yet knowing we had almost no chance of finding it. When we came upon a little island in the swamp, we decided to pitch a tent for the night.

Our clothes were never dry again for the entire time we were in the park. Never before or since have I been in terrain, not even in high alpine regions, where I felt nature to be so remorselessly hostile. Though it yielded almost every day vistas of matchless beauty, never once did I feel it offered them in friendship. After only five or six days, we were becoming demoralised, especially since we found only soft snow and no ice. We thought of little else but good food and warm, dry clothes. I remembered Bonatti's account of the Italian ascent of K2. After a time, he said, the climbers dreamt not of sexy young women, but of motherly fat ones who served them salads, pastas and fresh meat.

One day we decided to climb a mountain just above the hut. We decided to go directly to its main face, which meant first trekking through scrub. It took us nearly three hours to cover a kilometre or so, as we fought our way through the tangle of trees, branches lashing our faces, snow going down the sleeves of anoraks as we raised our arms to push the branches aside. Cursing nature for not allowing us

even on this day, after a wet and cold night, the relatively simple pleasure of climbing a nearby mountain, we made our way to the face and
were on the summit in late afternoon. There we enjoyed some choco-
late and a cigarette rolled painfully and slowly with frozen fingers.
The view of the park and its peaks, bathed in the crimson light of
the late afternoon sun, was one of heartrending beauty.

We headed down. The slope was steep but the snow was soft,
freshly fallen the night before, so we didn't rope up. My good
friend, Dave, with whom I had climbed many times, and who had
held me more than once when I fell on rock climbs, was perhaps
fifty to sixty metres ahead of me. He was having a pee near a bush
that protruded a metre from the snow. As I came down I slipped,
and started sliding a little in the snow, not dangerously because I
would not slide far in such soft snow. But because the snow was
fresh it was sticky and soon formed a small avalanche. When it
came near to Dave, I could see that it was already high enough to
sweep him off his feet. Not more than twenty metres behind him
was a cliff eighty or more metres high.

I sat and looked as the avalanche gained momentum and height.
Almost certainly, I thought, it would sweep Dave off his feet and
over the cliff where he would plunge to his death. Yet I looked on,
seeing it all as in slow motion and with detached amusement,
thinking what a way for him to go, with his climbing trousers down.
He grabbed the bush and the avalanche passed.

Not long after I saw a film on a climb of Everest by a British
team. Two climbers were making a bid for the summit, without
oxygen. The lead climber dropped onto the slope from exhaustion.
His friend, who had climbed with him for many years, thought he

was dead. He searched the pockets of his fallen comrade, looking for cashew nuts. Since he was dead, he thought, he may as well have his nuts. That's all. He thought nothing and felt nothing else.

When I spoke of the need that many mountaineers have to seek through climbing an understanding of their humanity I expressed sympathy for that need. My own sensibility has been profoundly shaped by it and by the effects of the landscape of my boyhood. I do not, however, believe that an interest of any kind in nature or animals is essential to a full development of one's humanity. In the modern celebration of nature and wilderness we are sometimes in danger of condescending to, even having contempt for, people who have no interest in nature, and who are in various ways physically incompetent. We are always vulnerable to the ideal of a full human life being a life in which, as Marx said, we read philosophy in the morning, work with our hands in the afternoon and fish in the evenings. But there are people who want only to work in philosophy, who never leave the city, who are completely incompetent when it comes to doing anything with their hands and who cannot bear animals. In a very important sense, their lives need be lacking in nothing. The English philosopher Stuart Hampshire said that anyone with some knowledge of other cultures and with an imaginative sense of human possibilities must realise that there are many but incommensurable ways of living. In a memorable phrase, he remarked that we all go lopsided to the grave. That's half true.

Norman Malcolm reports in *Wittgenstein: A Memoir* that when the philosopher was on his deathbed he asked his housekeeper to tell his friends 'that it has been a wonderful life'. Malcolm says he found it deeply moving that Wittgenstein should say this in the face of the evident misery that had marked much of his life. He did not, however, suggest that knowledge of that misery might give one reason to challenge what Wittgenstein said. Wittgenstein was not in any ordinary sense expressing an *assessment* of his life. He was expressing an unconditional gratitude for it. No one has the right to challenge him to qualify his gratitude.

There is no human being of whom we have the right to say that he or she could not express the same gratitude as Wittgenstein did. Only arrogant folly could make one think that someone who had all her life been estranged from the natural world could not, with lucidity, say that she had had a wonderful life.

Arrogance?

At the time when my father and I lived in the country with Jack and Orloff, we had a cow, Rusha, who gave us many calves all of whom we called Bimbo. My father killed one of them for meat. I did not see him do it. When he returned to the house after he had killed the calf, he was shaking. The sight of him troubled me for years to come. I knew he believed he had done something terrible. Because he was my father and because I was only seven years old, I could not believe that he could be so distraught and also mistaken about what .
he had done.

He was agitated for days afterwards. Though he did not talk about it to me, I overheard him speaking to my mother and to Hora's brother who had helped him kill the calf. From what I overheard I knew that he was ashamed of himself, but I also sensed that his agitation expressed something deeper than shame. For reasons that never became clear to me, my father and Hora's brother could not subdue the calf who struggled long and hard against them. My father was mortified, not so much because he killed the calf, but because he did not relent. He could not come to terms with the arrogance he showed in his refusal to yield. That he should prove to be such a man was the source of his shame. What went deeper was his belief that he had offended against something in the order of nature.

Earlier I said that his compassionate fatalism extended to all living things and even to the land that supported them when droughts cracked the earth, burnt the grass until it died and left the paddocks with little but dust in them. When he killed the calf that attitude had not fully developed in him although hints of it could be detected in his behaviour towards Jack and Orloff. Only after he went mad, and the terrors of madness made him taste the bitterness of affliction, did it deepen and become his defining orientation to the world. His response to the way he killed the calf was, I suspect, an intimation of what he was to become, an intimation of how he had offended against the pity he believed is owed to all living things. He never thought of his pity as merely a subjective attitude that he projected onto an objective world. He expressed it as though it were a faculty that revealed the world as it truly is. It was against the world, as pity revealed it to him, that he believed he had offended when he refused to relent.

Laments about human arrogance towards other forms of life are common and are themselves sometimes arrogant in the relish with which they mock what they take to be our vanity and our claims to dominion over nature. Such arrogance is a danger intrinsic to many forms of the lament because they are invariably made at some distance from our ordinary human concerns. Sometimes the distances are too great for anyone to distinguish the tones of

arrogance?

authentic human concern from those of the fat relentless ego. When the lament is from the standpoint of the universe, from where we seem like 'specks of dust', it is impossible to hear voices that are locally inflected as any voice must be if it is to reveal to our compassion the meaning of what we do and suffer. The conclusion should not be that therefore nothing matters objectively. It should be that the concept of something mattering, of something having meaning, can have no application from the point of view of the universe. From there neither the assertion nor the denial that anything matters makes sense.

Albert Schweitzer was affectionately mocked for trying to avoid treading on insects. He expressed his attitude to all living things including the microbes he saw under his microscope as Reverence for Life. He writes:

> To undertake to lay down universally valid distinctions of value between different kinds of life will end in judging them by the greater or lesser distance at which they seem to stand from us human beings—as we ourselves judge. But that is a purely subjective criterion. Who amongst us knows what significance any other kind of life has in itself and as part of the universe?

Admirable though Schweitzer was in many ways, this is foolish but not because he regrets killing microbes, although I confess it sounds a little wacky to me. I am conscious, however, that readers might feel the same about the self-reproach that I said one could sensibly feel for washing a spider down the plughole, or even for thoughtlessly crushing wildflowers. What I find foolish in his remarks is his claim that when he kills microbes in order to save human lives he makes a subjective judgment. From what perspective is it subjective?

Objective and subjective are words that easily get one into trouble, but it is, I think, uncontroversial that objectivity is a normative concept. It's a bad thing to fail to be objective, because only when one is objective can one 'see things as they are'. When Schweitzer apologises for, or makes some qualification to, his judgment because it is 'subjective', he appears to say either that an objective judgment might be at variance with it and show it up, or that there is no such thing as an objective judgment to be made. I think he meant the former, for if he meant that even in principle there can be no objective judgment, then, of course, there is no point in 'admitting', as though it were a defect, that one's judgment is the only kind of judgment there can be.

In discussions such as this it is good to keep one's feet on the ground, although, admittedly, that is not a good place from which to try to see things from the point of view of the universe. But it is the only place, I think, from which one can call someone—oneself included—to seriousness, to the kind of sobriety where one can require that someone stands behind his words so that he and others can know that he really means them, or even that the words he speaks have meaning, or if they do have meaning that one can say something serious by speaking them. 'From the point of view of the universe our concerns mean nothing' is, I suppose, a sentence whose words mean something, but when someone speaks those words, then, I think, he can say nothing serious with them in anything that looks like a genuine human interchange.

arrogance?

Each human life is precious. So, though differently, are animal lives and so, though again differently, are plants, trees, the country-side and wilderness. The point of saying that they are in their different ways precious is that all of them can, and have through the ages, inspired reverence, though the reverence shows itself in different ways in each case. Reverence for human life shows itself in the kind of limit other people are to one's will—the kind we express when we say that they possess unconditional rights or that they are ends in themselves. It shows dramatically in the remorse that a person feels when he has transgressed such limits and murdered another human being. We know that human beings can kill themselves after they have become murderers or accomplices to murder, and though we may wish that they didn't, though we may even condemn them for doing so, it is part of our understanding of what it means to murder another human being that we find it understandable that they should wish to kill themselves.

Earlier I quoted Isak Dinesen saying that all sorrows can be borne if you tell a story about them and I then entered a qualification of my admiration for that marvellous insight. Now I enter another and more radical one. Our response to immanent death oscillates between a sense of aloneness and the comfort found in the knowledge of a shared mortality, but the oscillation is not a sign of confusion. Only a corrupt remorse, however, can seek comfort in a community of the guilty. Remorse is radically individuating of the victim and also of the person who has wronged her. The moral despair that remorse can bring to the person who suffers it, despair that can lead them to commit suicide, is I think the psychological shadow cast by the fact that the guilty are radically singular, a shadow that obscures the clear vision necessary for lucid atonement. It is not even intelligible that a person should wish to kill himself because he had killed microbes or insects, and it would show moral failings rather than virtue if they should want to do it having killed an animal. Had my father tried to shoot himself days after he had killed the calf, then I would not have taken that as a sign of the depth of his pity for the calf, but as a sign that he had become unhinged.

Reflection on remorse, including of course reflection on its many corruptions, can teach us much about our understanding of what it means to wrong someone. The sober and lucid remorse of a person who is guilty of murder may, of course, be informed by a sense of reverence for life, or of the sanctity of life, but any account of what *that* comes to must focus on the fact that the offence is against a particular individual, and not against life, or the sacred in general. When the person who is remorseful exclaims in painful recognition of the meaning of what he has done, 'My God, what have I done?' any answer he or someone else would elaborate cannot be too general. The answer cannot be that he has violated the social contract, or that he has been a traitor to rationality, or that he has offended against the sanctity of life.

The reason is obvious: such an answer deflects attention from the individual who has been wronged. When the killing is of a human being, if the individual whom he has killed is not the focus of his remorse, then, whatever someone might mean by reverence for life, he will have missed what it means to have reverence for a human life, or to find it sacred. Whatever unity the word 'life' can bring to ethical responses to all living things, it will bring only distortion if one is not alert to the fact that 'life' is a word with many meanings.

arrogance?

When thinking about this, philosophers have been troubled by the way remorse focuses on the individual who was wronged. If Fred was murdered, the wrong would have been the same if it had been Tom. What makes murder terrible is not that it was of Fred or Tom, but that it was of a human being, or a person, or a rational agent, they say. The features of Fred that made him such a distinctive, colourful and loveable personality are irrelevant.

It is true. Fred's individuating features, the distinctive personality that would make him the glory of liberalism's celebration of individuality, are irrelevant to the moral terribleness of his murder. But that kind of individuality is not the kind that makes him irreplaceable in the sense that goes together with a conception of his preciousness. It is the idea that every human being, whatever their distinctive characteristics or lack of them, is precious and irreplaceable, that informs our sense of what it means to wrong them. The difference in our responses to animals is a function of the degree to which that kind of individuality is attenuated in them. Insects have no share in it at all which is why no one could seriously say they felt remorse because they washed the spider down the plughole, or even because they plucked the wings off flies.

Remorse is sometimes characterised as moral regret. If remorse is not the right word to describe how one feels when one reproaches oneself for washing the spider away, one might think that 'regret' is. But now, if one asks how regret for what one did to the spider differs from the regret that one broke a vase, even one that was of great sentimental value and therefore irreplaceable, the answer seems to be that regret over what one did to the spider is regret of an ethical kind. Does that mean it does not focus on the particular spider that was killed but only on some ethically reprehensible feature of one's character?

I think not. If one tried to teach a child not to wash spiders down the plughole, one would (should) not say, 'What matters is your character, not the spider.' If the spider didn't matter—that particular spider that was washed away—it's difficult to see what the worry could be about the child's character. Or, to put it another way, unless the child worried about that particular spider, then desisting from washing it away wouldn't have the desired effect on his character. Contrast this with the hypothetical person who scraped into nothing the blade of grass whose presence reawakened Hora's reverence for life. That blade of grass could not, I think, intelligibly be the focus of his regret or inform the character of his shame.

The importance we attach to the individual conceived of as irre-placeable, and its connection with our understanding of what it means seriously to wrong someone and the connection of both with what I have called the realm of meaning, shows itself often in life. Writing as I am in the aftermath of the terrorist attacks of September 11, I have often reflected why it is so disquieting to hear people say that 'they' don't value the individual the way we do. Do they mean that, whereas we in the liberal democracies value individualism as a political ideal, 'they' are much more collectivist in their ethics? No, the claim that 'they' don't value the individual in the way that 'we' do comes to much the same as the claim that human life doesn't matter to 'them' as it does to us. That is why 'they' can do such terrible things.

Who values individual life in the way 'they' don't? We of the civilised nations, it would seem. Who are 'they'? The suicide bombers, of course, but also, I think, the peoples from the countries

arrogance?

from where the bombers came—people with dark complexions who live, or who are thought to live, in poor, overpopulated countries.

I knew a woman when she was grieving over her recently dead son. She said of Vietnamese mothers she saw on television grieving over their children, killed by American bombing, 'It's different for them, they can just have more.' In *A Common Humanity: Thinking about Love & Truth & Justice*, I call her 'M' and I will do the same here. James Isdell, protector of the Aborigines in Western Australia, thought much the same about Aboriginal women whose children were taken from them. 'They soon forget their offspring,' he said, explaining why he 'would not hesitate for a moment to separate any half-caste from its Aboriginal mother, no matter how frantic her momentary grief might be.'

Isdell and M could not see that the victims of their racist denigration could be individuals in the sense in which we mean it when we say that all human beings are unique and irreplaceable, not just to those who care for them, but unique and irreplaceable, period. 'Our' children are irreplaceable, but 'theirs' are replaceable more or less as our pets are. That is what M and Isdell thought.

Remarks of the kind expressed by M and Isdell show how far racist denigration reaches: it reaches to everything 'they' say and do. Nothing—not their loves, their griefs, their joys, their hatreds—can go deep in 'them'. Someone who sees a people in that way cannot believe that 'they' can be wronged in the ways 'we' can be or as deeply as 'we' can be. In the most natural sense of the expression they see 'them' as 'less than fully human'.

167

We have no reason to believe that there are peoples or races who are as M and Isdell perceived the victims of their denigration to be—incapable of the relationships that in part condition and in part express our sense that every human being is unique and irreplaceable as nothing else we know in nature is. Acknowledgment of that is the most important aspect of the acknowledgment that all the peoples of the earth share a common humanity.

Often people say that if only we could see, and having seen remember, that at bottom all human beings are the same, then we would have reason to hope for a just world. There is truth in that, but only insofar as our perception of what we have in common goes beyond what M and Isdell conceded they had in common with the victims of their denigration.

They knew that, like them, Aborigines and Vietnamese form attachments, are mortal and vulnerable to misfortune, that they are rational, have interests, that indeed, they are persons. M and Isdell did not suffer from ignorance of what we ordinarily call facts about the victims of their denigration. They suffered from meaning-blindness. Although the grief of the women who had lost their children was visible and audible to them, they did not see in the women's faces or hear in their voices grief that could lacerate their souls, mark them for the rest of their days. They could not see that sexuality, death and the fact that at any moment we may lose all that gives sense to our lives can mean to 'them' what it does it us. But to see just that capacity in a people is a condition of seeing that their humanity is defined, as ours is, by the possibility of *ever deepening* responses to the *meaning* of facts of the human condition. It is that acknowledgment that lies behind the hope that the knowledge, full and in our hearts, that all

arrogance?

human beings are alike, would bring with it a desire for justice for all.

If M and Isdell were not meaning-blind, if it were true that Aborigines and Vietnamese were as they perceived them to be, then the distinction they drew between us and them would be a distinction that marked a genuine difference in kind between members of our species. It would not, of course, mean that Isdell's treatment of Aboriginal mothers would have been justified. One can consistently look upon Aborigines as Isdell saw them and still judge what he did to be cruel, though one could not believe that it constitutes the same kind of wrong against them as it would against us. Some white slave-owners admonished other white slave-owners for being cruel to their slaves while not believing for a minute—while not even finding it intelligible—that slavery itself constituted an injustice.

There is an important lesson to be learnt from reflection on M and Isdell. The things they readily attribute to those whom they believe they could not wrong as we wrong one another are exactly the things that constitute the raw materials for most theories about the nature of morality and of its authority over us. Yet, if I am right that no elaboration on what M and Isdell readily grant—that Aborigines and Vietnamese are persons, that they are rational beings, that they are beings with interests and desires and so on—can take one to an understanding of what it means for us to wrong one another, then it shows what we take for granted when we take any of those theories as serious contenders for the reflective characterisation, and sometimes the reconstruction, of our moral life. We take for granted exactly what those theories are forgetful of—the meaning of what it is to wrong someone. M and Isdell are meaning-blind. Theories that do not appreciate the significance of that fact are meaning-forgetful.

Animals lack almost entirely what M and Isdell were prepared to attribute to the victims of their racist denigration. That is one reason why we cannot wrong them when we are cruel to them as we would wrong a fellow human being to whom we are cruel. It is why we cannot wrong them when we kill them as we would wrong a human being if we murdered him. And that is why we speak so naturally of us and them, of human beings and animals, rather than human beings and other animals.

Creatureliness

When I was a student I had three female cats who, on one occasion, fell pregnant at the same time. Suddenly there were fourteen kittens in the house that I shared with other students. Sadly, within less than a week cat flu reduced their number to one. I could not tell whether the surviving kitten was lucky or cursed to have three neurotic mother cats caring for her. Whenever she wanted to do anything—even just to walk down the passage—she had to run the gauntlet of their frustrated affection. The first mother licked her so hard that she was flattened to the floor. After she picked herself up, her fur matted and wet, she would be lucky to walk half a metre before the second and then the third mother cat did the same. Sometimes she was lucky to get away with just her triple-licking. At other times it started all over again with her first mother coming in again after the third had exhausted herself satisfying her maternal urges. By this time the kitten looked as though she had been thrown in a pool of sticky fluid. She was not in good humour about it.

The four of them slept in a cupboard under the stairs. One day a blind woman visited with her dog, Jedda, a wonderfully good-natured and well-disciplined labrador. The cupboard door was open. Trained though she was, Jedda could not resist sniffing around it to confirm her suspicion that she had smelled cats. Three cats in mid-air with their teeth bared and their claws out was the first I saw of the calamity to come. They had sprung as one from the dark at the back of the cupboard. The frustrated maternal instinct that showed itself in their unrelenting licking now showed itself more dramatically in the ferocity of their attack on the dog. Clearly they intended to do as much harm to her as they could. Poor Jedda had no chance. Perhaps it was what remained of her discipline that caused her to hesitate or perhaps she was too shocked to move. At any rate she stood at the cupboard door long enough for the cats to wound her badly. When she fled howling out of the house and down the street she left her owner shaken and spattered with blood. The cats went back to the cupboard, looking annoyed that I had not protected them from the need do this.

More than anything else, perhaps, the sight of animals with their mothers inspires in us the wonder—in some people the disgust—of seeing ourselves in animals and seeing them in ourselves. Often we describe what we see in common between human and animal mothers as the expression of a maternal instinct, but in our ordinary ways of speaking we do not, I suspect, attach technical significance to that expression. We mean nothing much more definite than that it belongs to their creaturely nature to do this. But when we come to reflect on what we mean, deep cultural pressures drive us to say that the behaviour and feelings we referred to as common to human and animal mothers are the effect of biological causes of the kind that evolutionary theory looks into. And that, as is well-known, has generated fierce controversies, driven by political as well as theoretical considerations, about the relative roles played by nature and nurture in the explanation of human behaviour.

Presupposed but hardly ever questioned in that debate is the belief that the sciences of nature would deepen our understanding of whatever we should assign to nature, and that the social sciences would deepen our understanding of whatever we should assign to nurture. That belief is not, of course, groundless, but I think that there is much less truth in it than was assumed and certainly much less than either group of scientists hoped to discover. Indeed, in my judgment, the narrowed sense of possibilities that are entailed by it distorted our understanding of our creatureliness and so we lost more than we gained.

In part that was because the ideological drive behind some of those discussions led the sciences, especially the more popularising evolutionary theorists, in stridently reductionist directions. Both sides had their reasons for wanting to demystify values that many people had taken to be *sui generis*, and to see them instead as serving biological or social functions. The aggressive vulgarity of Desmond Morris's reminder that even astronauts have to piss is of a piece with the debunking spirit of his book *The Naked Ape*, common in the social-evolutionary literature of the time and since. This prophet from Regents Park Zoo in London undertook to rebuke us for taking ourselves and our cultural achievements too seriously and for forgetting that we are animals. The rhetorical point of much of the debunking was not merely to say that we are animals, some of whose behaviour can be explained by biological theories. It was to insist that we are animals *in our essence*.

Morris hoped to encourage us to embrace the fact that animality is at the heart of our human identity, but nothing in evolutionary theory can compel acceptance of what is animal in our nature. When Swift lamented, 'Celia shits,' he was not ignorant of the fact that she was obedient to a biological imperative and that she would die if she seriously resisted it. To tell him that the imperative is a fact of nature is like telling someone who visits his wife's grave each day that there is no point in it because the dead are dead and do not appreciate that one goes to their grave even when it is cold and raining. Neither is so much the compelling basis for an attitude, as just the *expression* of an attitude. In the one case the person could reply that he knows that his wife is dead, for why else should he be visiting her grave? In the other Swift could say that he knows Celia must shit, that there are good biological reasons for it, but that it is disgusting nonetheless.

Swift's visceral response was part of a larger web of meaning, just as disgust with sexuality was part of a view of the 'flesh'—a concept for which few people can find a place any more, and those who do have often been compelled to acknowledge that the language which would reveal its use to be anything but morbid has gone dead on them. The plausibility for us of psychological theories that make disgust with the body look necessarily like a pathology depends, I think, on a radical rearrangement of the conceptual space in which we make meaning of the body, rather than on an allegedly neutral account of the facts of our psychological and biological nature that would underwrite that rearrangement.

creatureliness

Does evolutionary theory have much to teach us about our feelings and behaviour? Because we are an evolved species, it is tempting to think that it must have. But there is no must about it, I believe. The only sensible thing to do is to look to see what it has achieved, but, of course, one's judgment of that will be a function of one's sense of its task. A very thin conception of what altruism is will make even the behaviour of soldier ants look altruistic. Descriptions of what needs to be explained can be tailor-made to suit even the thinnest explanatory concepts available. Never mind the discussions, for hundreds of years, of what it means to love one's neighbour. Those discussions, people like Morris think, are just the kind that need to be brought to earth by reminders about the biological necessities that operate even in astronauts. Or rather, to be fair, that's what one half of him thinks. The other half contemplates with impressive humility the complexity of animal behaviour and the uncanniness of the recognition of how often what we do seems just like what they do.

As an example of what I have in mind when I criticise the reductionist tendencies in much social-evolutionary theory, take the concept of behaviour modification. It's a good example because the concept straddles work in the biological sciences and in psychology. Does one understand better what one is doing, when one disciplines a child who selfishly makes family life impossible, by thinking that the child has behaviour problems and that one should try to find the best means to modify his behaviour?

Shall I punish him, bribe him, or ostracise him? Each of these descriptions refers not merely to an instrument which I might use to modify his behaviour, but to actions and what they can mean. Each implies a radically different relationship with the child, and the differences are in part moral. If I am his father I may have a right to punish him: if I am not, I may not. Either way, I would be likely to corrupt him if I bribed him, and I would corrupt his understanding of what he has done and the responses it may legitimately provoke if I encourage his brothers and sisters to ostracise him. And I would corrupt them too. These are, of course, moral considerations, but one should not think of them just as principles which would govern the choice of which behaviour modifying techniques I might deploy, thus leaving the concept of behaviour modification as the salient one with which to understand the task before me.

If, after reading an influential professor of educational theory, I decided to encourage his ostracism, someone might accuse me of having a corrupt and shallow understanding of family life. He might point out the baleful consequences for children of such ostracism, but to understand fully what it means to suffer those consequences and for a father to inflict them on his child, to understand the wrong as well as the harm I have done him, I must think in that realm of meaning where the content of what I consider will not be separable from its form. If the professor of education were to say that at bottom what I want is to modify his behaviour, I would deny it. What I want is for him to understand what he is doing and to understand what it means to other members of the family, to understand what obligations and what constraints his thoughtlessness imposes on me, his father. And more of course, but that is, I hope, enough to show that understanding proceeds in the direction of the particular, and by elaborating distinctions rather than blurring them. When it carries the connotations it possesses in ordinary English, the expression 'behaviour modification' implies manipulation, which is almost always unjust. When it tries to slough off those connotations, hoping to become a neutral term in a science of behaviour, hoping thereby to find in generality the deepened understanding that generality delivers in the hard sciences, then it impedes rather than advances understanding.

It is so with the understanding of people and also, I believe, with the understanding of animals. That is implied in the descriptions I have given of my relationships to animals and of what they do. It is why I endorsed and elaborated Vicki Hearne's suggestion that disciplining a dog is 'educating' it 'into citizenship', a process which requires one to distinguish commands given with rightful authority from those that are not and both from force. That distinction requires a substantive concept of respect for the dog's dignity, respect of the kind beautifully illustrated in Rush Rhees' account of his failure to discipline his dog, Danny. It is the respect I implied when I said that we disciplined Gypsy to make her trustworthy rather than just predictable. Hearne says that trainers who are committed to behaviouristic theories of what they do succeed despite those theories rather than because of them. When training becomes more or less accurately describable in behaviouristic terms, then it brutalises the animal. To see that none of this need be sentimental I will quote Hearne quoting with approval the great animal trainer William Koehler on 'humaniacs' who are:

'kindly' people, most of whom take after a 'kindly' parent or an aunt 'who had a dog that was almost human and understood every word that was said without being trained'...They often operate individually but inflict their greatest cruelties when amalgamated into societies. They easily recognise each other by their smiles, which are as dried syrup on yesterday's pancakes. Their most noticeable habits are wincing when dogs are effectively corrected and smiling approvingly when a dozen ineffective corrections seem only to fire a dog's maniacal attempts to hurl his anatomy within reach of another dog that could maim him in one brief skirmish. Their common calls are: 'I couldn't do that—I couldn't do that,' and 'Oh myyyy—oh myyyy.' They have no mating call. This is easily understood.

My discussion of the concept of behaviour modification is not intended to prove anything. I offer it only to suggest, firstly, that much of our understanding of human and animal behaviour cannot without serious distortion be abstracted from the realm of meaning into an impersonal realm of factual/scientific inquiry, and, secondly, that understanding in the realm of meaning often proceeds by moving to more particular and discriminating descriptions than to more general ones as happens in the natural sciences.

To answer the question of whether social evolutionary theory has helped us to understand ourselves and our relations to animals and to nature more generally, it is worth carrying that suggestion into other examples. Will the concept of pair-bonding help us to understand what we have celebrated in fidelity or, for that matter, in certain forms of promiscuity? Will the concept of territorial instinct show us what love of country can be and enable us rightly to distinguish it from jingoism? Will evolutionary theories of altruism tell us even a little about the nature of compassion for the severely afflicted, of its purity when all traces of condescension are absent from it, or of its power to reveal the full humanity of those whose affliction has made their humanity invisible? In any of these examples, can it help us to distinguish the reality of the virtue from its many false semblances? When someone calls upon us to reflect on what we have done when we have betrayed a faithful partner, or supported murderous policies because of a jingoistic allegiance to country, or when we gave money to a homeless person with undisguised condescension, will we turn to evolutionary theory to help us to understand?

It is inconceivable to me that there should be support in evolutionary theory for Socrates' claim that it is better to suffer evil than to do it. The Socratic ethic is an ethic of renunciation. It requires that we be prepared to renounce the only means to safeguard what is most precious to us and what we most deeply need if those means are evil. Socrates was told by almost everyone to whom he professed his ethic that he must be shameless to renounce not only the means to protect himself, but also the means to protect those who depend on him. Even if we do not agree with it, the Socratic ethic often shows itself in the ways dilemmas present to us. Our deliberation about the Socratic horn of those dilemmas will be unaffected by whether evolutionary theory speaks for or against it. If it speaks against—as in a way it has in the voice of Nietzsche—nothing compels us to take much notice. If it speaks for it, then it will always be for the wrong reasons. But in this matter acting for the right reasons, or perhaps better, in the right spirit, is of the essence.

Civilisation, said G. K. Chesterton, is suspended on a spider's web of fine distinctions. The spider's web is the realm of meaning.

Debunkers of all kinds long to tear it down. When presented with many and fine distinctions they grow impatient. There are many reasons for this and they depend on intellectual and moral temperament as much as on more theoretical considerations. One important reason is that many debunkers—people for whom an impulse to reductionism is second nature—long for something robust and they believe they will have it if they can reduce things to a commonsensical social purpose or ground them in a theory of their universal biological origins. These are 'at bottom' type of aspirations—at bottom all human beings are the same, at bottom what is sensible in morality aims at the human good, and so on. That is why many people have turned to social-evolutionary theory in the hope of finding there a trans-cultural, universal ethic.

Many times in this book I have emphasised that the realm of meaning cannot be underwritten by reason, that it is not 'part of the fabric of the universe', not a solid part of nature that must be acknowledged by anyone who has a concern for truth and a capacity to find it. Nothing makes claims to meaning true or false in the way that the fact that it is raining makes true the assertion that it is. F. R. Leavis said that the form of a critical judgment of a poem or novel is, 'It is so, isn't it?' and that the form of the response to it is, 'Yes, but...' It's a fine way of characterising the essentially conversational nature of judgments in the realm of meaning, their objectivity as well as their necessary incompleteness. Always, it is assumed, the text would be before the conversationalists, and the never-ending 'Yes but...' requires that one remain open to it, in a responsiveness that is both vital and disciplined by the critical concepts constitutive of thought in the realm of meaning. That is why Leavis was right to resist philosophers who said that it should be possible, *a priori*, to list the criteria that distinguish good from bad critical responses. It is no different in life. We cannot tell in advance what is possible in the realms of meaning, because we cannot say what vital responsiveness, disciplined by and disciplining a language 'used at full stretch', will reveal to us.

The fineness of the web irritates some people. Its fragility unnerves them.

Attempts to explain and also to reconstruct our deepest values by looking to evolutionary theory belong to a family of ethical theories that assume that those values serve purposes. It is a natural thought, especially if one takes those values to be prescriptive in their essence, to guide conduct by means of rules or principles to the achievement of an assumed end—the human good, for example. Natural though that assumption is, there is a simple, and to my mind decisive, objection to it. Put in a slogan, it is that morality does not serve our purposes but is the judge of them. It 'supervenes upon purpose as an additional principle of discrimination' said the Welsh philosopher J. L. Stocks. If, for example, one's purpose is to live with as little conflict as possible, then one will devise strategies for doing so. Which of these one chooses will in the first instance be determined by one's assessment of their value in achieving one's purpose. That—judging efficient means to ends—is the application of one principle of discrimination, the one that is part of the very concept of purpose. There will be others, but when they have had their say morality enters as judge. Some means are efficient but cruel; some are less efficient but bring additional pleasure in their train, which would be fine except that the pleasures may be corrupt. But in order to determine which means are decent to use one cannot look to the end which decency serves, for there is no such end. Were one to suggest, for example, that the essence of decency is to serve the end of social co-operation, then one will discover that it is decency—or more generally morality—that is the judge of which forms of social co-operation can decently be enjoyed And so it is with any end that morality is alleged to serve, be it individual flourishing or happiness, the collective good, or even the survival of the species—morality will judge which forms of them, and which means for their achievement, are acceptable to a decent conscience.

Reflecting on M will again be instructive, I hope. Evolutionary ethics can at best deal only with what M acknowledges as existing in common between her and the Vietnamese. She knows she belongs to the same species as they do, but that does not give her reason to find depth in what they do and suffer. The sense of common humanity from which she excludes them is constituted not by facts of a kind available to socio-biological inquiry, but by meaning, by what it means to have and to lose children, to love and to mourn someone faithfully.

'Don't you see what you are doing!' M might say to someone whom she acknowledges as 'one of us' but who is superficial enough to try to have another child in just the spirit M attributes to the Vietnamese but finds impossible for herself. But in calling that woman to seriousness about what it means to be a mother who has lost a child, M would not remind her of the biological facts that she knows to be common between her and 'her kind' and the

Vietnamese. And she would see no point in rebuking the Vietnamese because, unlike her white friend who is contingently shallow, they (she thinks) are intrinsically incapable of understanding how degrading it is to be someone who can 'just have more'. Evolutionary theory may have something to say about why we are creatures who become attached to one another in ways that partially condition the kind of individuality that transcends the distinctions we make when we refer to people's individuating features, but from M's point of view that could not explain why we grieve, really grieve, whereas they 'grieve'. Her sense of her difference from the Vietnamese, a sense that depends on her seeing them as being incapable of fully appreciating the kind of individuality that deepens her grief as for someone who is unique and irreplaceable, is a sense of difference that depends on what culture rather than biology has made of that individuality.

Even if it were true, therefore, that one could derive simply from consideration of what it means to be a person (M has no doubt that the Vietnamese are persons and rational agents) imperatives that would be binding on all persons or rational agents and that accord with the imperatives we call 'moral', one would still not have conveyed what it means to fail (morally) to rise to them. What it means to wrong someone in a way that M finds unintelligible that 'we' could wrong 'them', will still be—I suspect entirely—unaccounted for. That is why it is probably no accident that philosophers who operate only with what M can grant to the Vietnamese constantly appeal, despite themselves, to expressions whose associations in natural language go far beyond the conceptual resources allowed by their theories. Instead of speaking only of persons or rational agents, for example, they will avail themselves of the rich associations that attach to our ways of speaking of human beings and of our shared humanity. Naturally one wonders what is really doing the conceptual work. M's example tells us.

Does the emphasis I place on the realm of meaning (which I acknowledge to be a cultural gift) commit me to the nurture side of the nature/nurture controversy? I don't believe that it does. Both parties to the debate assumed that biological science would deepen our understanding of whatever we rightly assigned to nature and that evolutionary theory would explain the biological causation of many of our feelings and much of our behaviour. But understanding our creatureliness, I have suggested, should focus not on the biological causes of our behaviour mostly hidden to us until science uncovers them, but on the body's part in the constitution of our concepts and on what we have made of the body in the realm of meaning.

Here is an example which I hope will explain what I mean.

It is a familiar fact that children who have been adopted some-times seek to find their natural parents and that they describe themselves as being in search of their identity. Sometimes a child whose father deserted her seeks him for the same reason though she knows the relationship between him and her mother went no further than a one-night stand, that he showed no interest in her upbringing and did not even inquire about her welfare. From the standpoint of moral or other conceptions of responsibility one might say he was no father. Yet, interestingly, the word is never fully withdrawn. Indeed, in this context, the accusation, 'You call yourself a father!' would have no point unless he were a father. And though we now distinguish between adoptive or step-fathers and biological fathers, there is still a strain in thinking of a person as having two fathers, a strain that places pressure on the adoptive or step-father not to press his claim to the title too strongly, qualified though the claim is. (Some people refer to the adoptive father as 'dad' and refuse to call him 'father'.)

It strikes me as a kind of moralisation of parenthood to think that the virtues of a devoted step- or adoptive 'father' are best acknowledged by saying that he rather than the irresponsible natural father is the real father. I suspect we do it because, though we are offended by the abdication of responsibility on the part of a father who had a one-night stand and then deserted mother and child, we are even more offended (or perhaps frightened) by the apparent irrationality of the fact that sleeping with a woman and making her pregnant could matter so much *of itself*. Yet though Oedipus' father was no model of responsible fatherhood, we understand Oedipus' horror when he discovers that he slew him:

> Now, shedder of father's blood,
> Husband of mother, is my name;
> Godless and child of shame,
> Begetter of brother-sons;
> What infamy remains
> That is not spoken of Oedipus.

Recently people have begun to seek the men who donated the sperm with which their mothers were inseminated. Sometimes they do it for the good practical reason that they want to know their genetic inheritance. Sometimes, however, they seek to find the sperm donors in order to understand who they are in the same spirit in which adopted or deserted children seek their natural fathers. In all the accounts I have read of this by the children themselves, seeking the sperm donors who impregnated their mothers, there is a sense of confusion and pathos, as though they know that they are in need of something that they can never have. They need to find their father, but they cannot think of a sperm donor as really a father. 'You call yourself a father? You're nothing but the sperm donor!' That is how a child deserted by her natural father might express her pain to him, finding rhetorical support in our ordinary ways of speaking which record our inclination to deny that to be a sperm donor is to be a father.

On the face of it, it seems irrational that it should matter so much how the mother was inseminated. On the one hand, a woman is inseminated through the natural sexual act and that gives to her deserted child a father who can be integral to the child's sense of identity. On the other hand, a woman is artificially inseminated, brings a child into the world, yet that child has no father.

The appearance of irrationality is heightened, I think, by the use of the word 'insemination': it is tailor-made to render irrelevant just those differences that distinguish becoming pregnant after having sex with someone from becoming pregnant by courtesy of a sperm donor. 'Becoming pregnant' is a more neutral expression than 'becoming inseminated' which is, as it were, immediately to one side of it and heading fast in the direction of medical and other scientific descriptions. To the other side is an expression like 'of your own flesh and blood', as that might be used when the pregnant mother laments the fact that her lover is indifferent to the fact that what she now carries is of his own flesh and blood.

Though its origins pre-date modern scientific developments, 'of my flesh and blood' is not a pre-scientific expression in the pejorative sense that we would use it more lucidly if our understanding were deepened by the science of genetics. On the contrary: when one takes it from its natural home in the realm of meaning into that of the impersonally factual, one deprives it almost entirely of the power to aid understanding. If a sperm donor were to meet the child that resulted from his donation, could he say, 'I am your father. You are my child, my own flesh and blood'? Only, I think, if his efforts to deceive himself about what he had done were helped along by a tin ear.

Yet, it is hard to say in advance what can and what cannot find its way into the realm of meaning. We cannot say in advance what children, mothers and sperm donors will make of their relations because it is not for abstract philosophy, psychology or some other science to say. It depends almost entirely on how they can creatively, and with integrity and lucidity, speak of who they are and what they have done. But the fact that this is a question to be settled is of itself testimony to the difficulty we have in thinking of a sperm donor as a father. The more neutral, social-working term— 'biological father'—has not, I think, achieved what people hoped it would. It is a term that sits unhappily between 'sperm donor' and 'natural father'. Because of its proximity to 'natural father' the expression 'biological father' acquired many of the associations that have accrued in the realm of meaning to the former, and that has enabled adopted children to seek their natural father while describing their quest as for their biological father. Those associations have not yet extended to 'sperm donor' and no one knows whether they ever will sufficiently for the expression to acquire, or to engage with expressions that have, the kind of depth needed for it to play a part in a child's understanding of its identity.

I have deliberately not considered what to say when the donor is also the woman's lover and rears the child with her. What one says about that will of course be a function of what one says of the other.

Yet I must admit that, even if one grants that the important distinctions we make are more or less as I have drawn them, the question of why we have made them will remain to be answered. Nothing I have said diminishes their apparent irrationality.

I am tempted to say the reason why we are reluctant to call a sperm donor a father is because sex, although it may be treated casually, is never intrinsically casual. But 'intrinsically casual' and 'intrinsically meaningful' are not expressions likely to yield clarity. I certainly don't mean that sex must always be 'deep and meaningful', or to deny that it can be for nothing but the pleasure of it and enjoyed just that way by both parties in a one-night stand. But there is a difference between a one-night stand that is open to the complex and often messy human entanglements that sex, of its nature, may unexpectedly throw up and one that refuses to be answerable to such possibilities. In saying that sex is never intrinsically casual, I meant to say that condemnation of the latter is not moral condemnation in the light of standards external to sexuality, but rather condemnation in the light of standards internal to it. An analogy might be helpful. The requirement that parental love be unconditional is not a requirement imposed from outside, by morality for example, but a requirement that makes parental love what it is and distinguishes if from its false semblances.

The idea that sex has depth intrinsically, as opposed to the idea that it is intrinsically casual and that we make something of it in particular relationships, is in many ways foreign to us, yet it shows itself, I think, in our condemnation of rape.

We think of rape as terrible in ways which can only be appreciated if we assume that a woman's sexuality can be precious to her. If sexuality were properly seen as essentially an instrument of pleasure and other purposes, as an instrument which can, contingently, bring something more serious in its train, or introduce us to something more serious (in the way money can introduce us to beauty), then it would be hard to see why rape should not be judged as a species of assault, or as something which could adequately be characterised in some variant of the thought that a woman has exclusive rights to her body. Then rape would be like the theft of a gold tooth, or like cutting off someone's finger to get their ring. Considered as a violation of autonomy, of a person's right over her body, or as a species of assault, rape would often be less serious than many muggings. Quite rightly, nobody thinks that.

We will not get closer to what we need, however, by saying that rape is a species of assault aggravated by psychological trauma, because the question naturally arises as to why a relatively minor assault should occasion such trauma. Rape is not terrible because trauma is added to physical injury. The nature of the trauma is conditioned by the distinctive terribleness of rape, by what rape means. Whether or not it is physically brutal, rape is violation of woman's sexual being. Because there would be no rape if there were genuine consent, we tend to focus on the consent, and therefore to see rape, wrongly, as in essence a particular violation of autonomy aggravated by physical injury.

The power of sex to make us feel things we never thought it possible to feel and to behave in ways we never dreamed we could (for good and for ill) has baffled people ever since they began to think about it. Biology plays only a small part in this, I think, because the power of sex over us, its capacity to drive us mad, even to make murderers of us, as much as its joyful sublimity, is a function of the fact that the joy and the madness depend on a culturally deepened conception of the uniqueness of individuals. Or perhaps better: the sublime and the demonic power of sex and that conception of individuality are interdependent.

Only in the last twenty years or so have we thought we could control the awesome power of sex with a set of prescriptions derived from the requirement that we respect the autonomy of persons. But of course what one is answerable to even in a one-night stand can always transcend anything that one had reasonably agreed to beforehand, anything that appears to be 'objectively' reasonable (to a court of law for example). It is inherent to sexuality as we have known it at least since Homeric times that one's partner in an otherwise casual relationship, apparently protected by a forest of agreements to the effect that nothing is to be taken too seriously, might fall dangerously in love, or even become deranged by obsessive jealousy. Then one is answerable despite all previous disclaimers.

The desire for sex without the risk of human entanglement, for a contract to expunge all answerability, is what people often seek in sex with prostitutes. Even then it is an illusion, but the readiness of the prostitute and her client to participate in such a delusion is one reason why prostitution has been thought to be intrinsically degrading to the prostitute and even more to her client. That is why prostitution functions so well as metaphor for the degradation of other things of intrinsic worth—the degradation, for example, of our need of truth by intellectual dilettantism. The answerability that I am trying to give expression to goes deeper than social responsibility and deeper even than moral responsibility. Cora Diamond has said that our practices of respecting the dead and giving names rather than numbers to our children are not so much moral practices as practices that are the source of morality. Much the same is true, I think, of our answerability to the emotional and spiritual turmoil—both wonderful and sometimes truly awful— that can develop from the most casual sexual relationships.

The need human beings have of each other, often unfathomable, is partly constitutive of and partly expressive of the individuality that we express when we say that human beings are unique and irreplaceable. Perhaps nowhere do the need and the individuality with which it is interdependent show themselves so powerfully and sometimes dramatically as in sexual relations. A philosopher, D. A. Richards, said that we should love people only 'on the basis of traits of personalities and character related to acting of moral principles'. Even though our attachment-based conception of individuality sometimes conflicts with morality, it is nonetheless what is best in it, and we would undermine it severely if we were to follow Richards' advice. More obviously still, we would undermine the unconditional love of parents for their children and I suspect not even Richards would believe that to be an edifying prospect. The foolishness of his remark will I hope be evident, but there is I think a similar moralising foolishness and small-spiritedness in the belief that one can legitimately protect oneself by means of quasi-contractual arrangements from the unpredictable human risks that are inseparable from every sexual relationship.

Because even the most casual sexual relationship renders its participants answerable to each other's needs and their (sometimes calamitous) consequences, and because needful attachment and our answerability to it play such a profound part in our sense that human beings are unique and precious, the location of our origins in the sexual act can go so deep with us that it can be fundamental to our sense of who we are. The connection between sex and identity is a function of sex's capacity to go deep, which is in turn a function of the way it involves us with others. People think of themselves as heterosexuals or homosexuals, but no one thinks of him or herself in the same sense as a masturbator. Being a masturbator is not a possible form of sexual identity.

It would not be so, I suspect, were it not for the physical details of sexuality. It would not be the same if women routinely became pregnant without the man's entry to their body and if routinely that entry aroused no pleasure and affection. It would not be so, I suspect, were it not for all the fleshy detail of attraction and arousal, if our bodies were not soft to the touch, inviting tender caresses, if we did not seek out other human beings for warmth and comfort and if we did not have faces to look into or avoid.

It matters too that a child can be loved before it is born and that the love is made possible—mediated—by the pleasure that the

creatureliness

mother (and others) can take in the changes in her body, changes which appear to us as beautiful. In the perception of that beauty, love becomes concrete and finds its tender expression. I doubt that a foetus growing in a glass jar on the mantelpiece could be an object of loving tenderness, though it would, of course, be a focus of concerned attention. Indeed it is the celebration in our art of a love mediated by the changes in a woman's body that has given sense to the expression 'being with child'. That—like 'of my own flesh and blood'—is an expression in the language of love and is misunderstood when it become the focus of contentious philosophical, theological or scientific theorising about the 'objective' properties of the foetus. The foetus is something that can rightly be loved, love made lucid by language which shows up not only love's false semblances, but also other responses, such as resentment, for example. It is astonishing how many people find that of less importance than whether the foetus is a rational being.

To return the body to the realm of meaning, to rescue it from the meaning-impervious nature of quasi-medical terminology that surrounds sex for medical, political and moralistic reasons has been an urgent concern of some latter-day feminists. It is interesting that the feminists' reclamation of a language to rescue female sexuality from various meaning-free zones cannot be prescriptive in the way that efforts to establish gender-neutral language were. A committee can (in principle) prescribe that we all use 'chairperson' rather than 'chairman', but no committee can prescribe 'cunt' as an alternative to 'vagina' or 'fuck' as an alternative to 'sexual intercourse', not because it would be morally inappropriate, but because the alternatives to 'vagina' and 'sexual intercourse' have to make their way in our living

speech. Some people object to 'four letter words' because they find
them an offence to modesty. Modesty conceived as a virtue has
been fundamental to most forms of opposition to the claim that
sex is intrinsically casual. But modesty should defend itself within
the realm of meaning, rather than fearfully retreating into quasi-
medical terminology. When it severs contact with the language of
love, modesty looks childish.

Through a kind of naturalism of surfaces deepened by literature
we explore our creaturely nature. We make something deep of
surfaces. It is in the imaginative appreciation of surface similarities
between the bodies of pregnant women and animals, and in the
surface similarities of their behaviour, rather than in the investiga-
tion of biological causes of maternal behaviour, that we discover
the creaturely nature we have in common. When we look more
closely at our behaviour and the behaviour of animals, however, we
also see important differences that are revealed in the fact that our
behaviour, but not that of animals, is often determined by reflection
on its meaning.

A human mother, neglectful of her children, may feel shamed by
the sight of a cat caring devotedly for her kittens, but reflection on
the biological basis of the cat's behaviour and of hers will not take
her far in understanding her failing as a mother. The ferocity with
which the mother cats attacked Jedda in order to protect the one
kitten remaining to them, and the causes of it in their evolutionary
history have little to tell us about the requirements that fall upon
mothers to care for their children. What will knowledge of that
evolutionary history tell us about the requirement to love our children unconditionally? The concept of unconditional love has no

application to animals, no matter how devotedly they care for their young or how ferociously they protect them at risk to their own lives. We can love unconditionally only because we can impose—consciously or unconsciously—conditions on our love and be answerable for the fact that we do it. We might impose them unconsciously, if for example we reject a child because she is a girl, or consciously if the child does not measure up to our expectations, especially moral expectations. When one reflects on what we must rise to in order really to be parents, then one realises those requirements are part of what it means to be a father or a mother. This is so whenever we are called upon to rise to the standards that distinguish the real from the counterfeit in certain virtues or affective responses—love, courage, grief, kindness and so on. Even in our creatureliness, therefore, we find both what we have in common with, and what distinguishes us from, animals.

Human Beings and Animals

When people say, as Schweitzer did, that the distinctions I have been making are subjective, are from the human point of view, it looks as though they want us to qualify the categorical nature of those distinctions. I am puzzled, however, by what I should do by way of such qualification. I readily grant that what I have called the realm of meaning, where I believe our ethical thought is embedded, does not exist in the nature of things, in the 'fabric of the universe' as one philosopher describes the place where values should reside if they are genuinely objective. The realm of meaning is of human origin, indeed a gift of culture which we might not care for, or reject, or neglect. Nothing whatsoever compels us to value it. Nothing in reason or in science underwrites it. But it would be a misuse of the natural meaning of the terms to say that therefore it is an artefact, or an invention, or even that it is a creation.

Acknowledging that the realm of meaning is a gift of culture does not diminish my certainty that the murder of a human being is more terrible than the killing of any animal and differently terrible in kind. I have heard people say that meat is murder, but I have not met anyone whom I credit with believing it. No one I know or have even heard of treats people who eat meat as though they are murderers or accomplices to murder. Most of the vegetarians I know are not pacifists. Were human beings slaughtered as often as animals are they would take up arms against those who are doing it and the governments that allow it. Yet most people do not get up from the table when meat is served. Some have been convinced of their obligations to become vegetarians by philosophers who tell them that it is worse to kill some animals than it is to kill an infant, yet none, I think, would respond to someone who served up infants in the way they do to someone who serves up animal flesh, even if those infants had died naturally.

I do not say any of this to mock vegetarians and I take none of it to be even the beginning of an argument against vegetarianism, an argument that I have, anyhow, no wish to prosecute. I say it in the spirit of urging sobriety in a discussion of whether it is arrogant to say that human beings are precious in the way that no other creature is. There are, I know, people who have endangered the lives of people working on animals in laboratories, but none has yet issued a call to arms of a kind one would expect if we discovered that human beings were being treated as vivisectionists treat animals.

It is true my appeal to sobriety relies on how we now behave and respond, but can anyone even seriously wish that we should respond otherwise? Can anyone seriously say they have been so thoroughly conditioned, indeed corrupted, by the prejudice of their times that they cannot act as though they believed that meat is murder but wished that they could? I don't believe it. Seriously to believe that one has been conditioned to respond in a certain way is also to wish that one could step back from one's conditioned responses in order to assess them. In this case that means seriously to consider that perhaps one should respond in ways appropriate to the belief that one lives amongst murderers and accomplices to mass murder.

One could go on in the same way. 'For a dog?' I asked when I reflected on how much I would spend on Gypsy's vet fees, and I admitted that I did not know how much, but I knew that I would not deprive the children of important medical care. People can argue about where to draw the line in a situation like that, but I know of no one whose dog would be treated as equal to a seriously sick infant. If someone did treat their dog like that I would not think of them as a pioneer of ethical thought, but as someone whose sentimentality had made them wicked. Thus, whatever point there is in saying that our attitudes to animals and to insects is human-centred, or subjective, it cannot seriously be to justify the charge that only arrogance or thoughtlessness could lead one to the kinds of judgments I have confidently claimed we make and would never wish not to make.

Are we therefore at the centre of the universe? There is no flat answer to that. We are precious as nothing else we know in nature and the moral of my call to sobriety is that there is no point in qualifying that with an empty 'from our, human, point of view'. On the other hand there is such a thing—a beautiful thing—as disinterested love of nature, even of inanimate nature, and that love can limit our will in a way that looks like the kind of limit that people have in mind when they talk of rights. I think it foolish to talk of the rights of trees or even of spiders, but that is partly because I think it is mistaken to talk of rights in the case of human beings.

To say that an action is unjust because it violates someone's rights adds nothing, I believe, to saying that it is unjust, neither by way of explaining why it is unjust, nor by making it more objectively or more stringently binding on the will. Of course this is controversial and I don't want even to begin to defend it. I mention it in the hope that it might reduce any offence caused by my claim that it is foolish to attribute rights to trees and mistaken to attribute them to animals. (For some people, I know, it will merely compound the offence.)

I have tried to show how an understanding of what it means to betray someone, to be cruel to them, to destroy wantonly animal, insect or even plant life, can create necessities and impossibilities for the will that are different in kind from the necessities of force, including psychological force. Elaboration which reveals what it means to be cruel to a human being or to an animal, and whose appreciation makes some actions impossible and others necessary, need not, I believe, mention rights. And, though this may again offend some people, my claim that at the deepest point of our ethics there is a conception of individuality that is groundless, formed from our attachments, justified neither by reason nor merit, deepened in love and made to seem more tractable in a language of rights and obligations—that claim might persuade others that I do not intend to demean the natural world when I say much the same about it. Attachment to animals and a disinterested love of nature are, I think, at the heart of anything that looks like an obligation to either.

Talk of rights in human affairs has had two functions. The first, which I have just mentioned, is theoretical—to explain why certain wrongs are wrongs, and (often) to ground them objectively. The second is moral. It constitutes one of the most noble fictions in our moral thought. Good-hearted people find it intolerable that just treatment of the powerless should depend on the generosity—on the charity in the old-fashioned sense—of the powerful. Since at least 1789, the refusal to accept it has driven the rhetoric of human rights in a noble attempt to bestow dignity on the powerless by creating the impression that rights are a kind of moral force field, a metaphysical barrier to the indignity of being crushed ruthlessly. 'I don't need your charity. I don't need your justice. I stand by my rights and demand that they be acknowledged.' That is the spirit of 1789.

It is an illusion. Unless an appeal to rights has force to back it, an appreciation of the wrong being protested depends entirely on a spirit of justice in those to whom the appeal is made. That appreciation need not—I think should not—include the concept of rights.

In her beautiful essay, 'Human Personality', Simone Weil writes:

If you say to someone who has ears to hear: 'What you are doing to me is not just', you may touch and awaken at its source the spirit of attention and love. But it is not the same with words like 'I have the right...' or 'you have no right to...' They evoke a latent war and awaken the spirit of contention...

If someone tries to browbeat a farmer to sell his eggs at a moderate price, the farmer can say: 'I have the right to keep my eggs if I don't get a good enough price.' But if a young girl is being forced into a brothel she will not talk about her rights. In such a situation the word would sound ludicrously inadequate.

No-one has written so beautifully and so hard-headedly about justice as Weil has because, I believe, no one has written so hard-headedly about affliction and the way in which the full humanity of those who suffer severe and degrading forms of it become invisible to other human beings. In 'Forms of the Implicit Love of God' she writes:

The supernatural virtue of justice consists of behaving exactly as though there were equality when one is the stronger in an unequal relationship. Exactly, in every respect, including the slightest details of accent and attitude, for a detail may be enough to place the weaker party in the condition of matter which on this occasion naturally belongs to him, just as the slightest shock causes water which has remained liquid below freezing point to solidify.

If the spirit of renunciation expressed in those fine remarks were to extend to our relations to animals and to nature, would we need a concept of rights in order to set limits to human arrogance?

When I was a boy living in the country my friends hunted rabbits and sold them in a nearby town. Embarrassed that I did not, I took my father's rifle and went to a nearby hill to shoot rabbits for our dinner and for Orloff. This is how I tell it in *Romulus, My Father*.

> I reached the hill in the mid-afternoon. For the first time in my life I was really alive to beauty, receiving a kind of shock from it. I had absorbed my father's attitude to the country-side, especially to its scraggy trees, because he talked so often of the beautiful trees of Europe. But now, for me, the key to the beauty of the native trees lay in the light which so sharply delineated them against a dark blue sky. Possessed of that key, my perception of the landscape changed radically as when one sees the second image in an ambiguous drawing. The scraggy shapes and sparse foliage actually became the foci for my sense of its beauty and everything else fell into place—the primitive hills, the unsealed roads with their surfaces ranging from white through yellow to brown, looking as though they had been especially dusted to match the high, summer-coloured grasses. It seemed to have a special beauty, disguised until I was ready for it; not a low and primitive form for which I had to make allowances, but subtle and refined. It was as though God had taken me to the back of his workshop and shown me something really special. It was inconceivable to me that I should now shoot a rabbit.

The impossibility that I expressed when I said that it was incon-ceivable that I should now shoot a rabbit is not a psychological impossibility. Sometimes we say we cannot do something, meaning that we couldn't do it no matter how hard we tried. In such cases if someone suggested that we try, we might say there is no point, but we would not also say it was a senseless suggestion, one that misunderstood what we meant when we said it was impossible for us to do the thing in question. A person might say, for example, that though he has no objections to killing chickens he cannot do it because every time he tries he feels sick. To him someone might say, 'It's not so bad if you shut your eyes,' or, 'It's easier if you chop their heads off than if you wring their necks.' The same is true of someone who volunteers for military service in a just and necessary war, but finds that he cannot kill another human being even though he thinks he should do it.

Sometimes, however, when we say that we cannot do something, we would reject the suggestion that perhaps we could if we tried as showing a misunderstanding of what we meant. That is how I would have responded if someone had been with me on that hill and said that I had come to shoot rabbits and that although he could understand that my experience been profoundly emotional, I should try to do what I had come there to do.

'Here I stand. I can do no other,' said Luther in the most famous expression of moral impossibility. I'm disinclined, however, to call my realisation that I could not, that afternoon, shoot a rabbit, a realisation that it was then morally impossible for me. It did not mean that I thought others should not kill rabbits, nor that if they understood what they were doing they could not. It did not even imply that I should not shoot rabbits the next day. But it did imply that, if I did shoot them the next day, I could not shoot them in the same spirit in which I would have before my experience on the hill.

A hard-nosed person might say that it makes no difference to the rabbit if you shoot it only after saying three Hail Marys or if you

shoot it with sadistic pleasure. The same person might be astonished that my father could think it mattered more that he killed the
calf without relenting than that he killed it.

In *A Common Humanity* I say that no human being, no matter how
foul their actions or their character might be, can rightly be killed in
the spirit of ridding the world of vermin. I called this an expression
of absolute value. A student responded by saying that perhaps
'vermin' should never be killed in the spirit of ridding the world of
vermin. Perhaps he was right. He was certainly right to raise the
question: is it not wrong to kill anything in a spirit of contempt for
it? Reason cannot, I think, answer that question. There are holy men
in India and in other places who respond to the world as though
nothing is deserving of their contempt. They have metaphysical
justification for this, someone will say, and metaphysical justifica-
tions can be assessed by reason. Perhaps they have such reasons,
although even if they have them I suspect they cannot fully explain
their behaviour, fully explain its colouration. But if someone told
me that Pablo Casals acted that way, I would have no trouble
believing it. The extract I quoted would be enough for me to believe
it. I would look no further for an explanation.

In his essay 'Looking Back at the Spanish War', George Orwell
tells the story that when he was sitting in the trenches he saw an
enemy soldier running across a parapet not far from him. He took
aim and was about to fire when he noticed that the man was
holding up his trousers. 'I had come here to shoot at "Fascists",'
Orwell said, 'but a man who is holding up his trousers is not a
"Fascist", he is visibly a fellow creature, similar to yourself, and you
do not feel like shooting at him.'

Orwell doesn't say he couldn't shoot the man. He says, 'you do not feel like shooting at him.' But that is, I think, intentionally an understatement, motivated perhaps by his sensitivity to the common belief that if one doesn't think that morally one ought not to shoot a man with his pants down then the feeling that one cannot *must* be expression of a psychological incapacity. It is certainly true that Orwell enunciated no generalisable principle about shooting men when they are holding up their pants. Tomorrow, in fact, he might shoot just such a man, even that same man. But it would be wrong to say that though Orwell's response was understandable—even heart-warming—it was a psychological rather than a moral response.

Orwell could just as well have said that he couldn't shoot that man with his trousers down and reject any suggestion that he might try as a foolish misunderstanding of what he meant. His response was interdependent with his coming to see that fascist soldier as a human being just like himself—a fellow human being, with all the moral resonances of that expression. That perception made it impossible for Orwell to shoot him at that time, just as my percep-tion of the beauty of nature made it impossible for me to shoot rabbits that afternoon. But if Orwell were to remain true to his perception of the soldier as his fellow human being then the spirit in which he continued as a soldier would be different. That would of course have to show itself in his conduct, but how, exactly, is not determined by his finding it impossible, on that occasion, to shoot a man holding up his trousers.

Some people—increasingly younger people, I suspect—become vegetarians because they find they cannot eat meat. At first they might not eat it for a practical reason—perhaps they are somewhere

human beings and animals

where the meat is very expensive or where the cooking is terrible—
and then gradually they find the very thought of eating meat
repulsive. It would be wrong to say of the vegetarians I am thinking
of that they had just become squeamish, if that meant that their
disgust was not a moral disgust. Asked to try to eat meat because,
for example, it would be much easier for those who cook the family
dinner, or because they do not eat enough protein to make up for
the absence of meat in their diet, they might say that their revulsion
is not of that kind. But because they are likely to identify the moral
basis of vegetarianism with decisions of principle, they might hesitate to say that theirs is a moral revulsion. And if, quite literally,
they can't eat meat because the mere thought of it makes them
nauseated, then they might be misled into believing that they
cannot eat meat only because of the sheer strength of a 'merely'
psychological revulsion against it. That would be a pity for, as it was
with Orwell, the impossibility they express is interdependent with a
perception of what it means to eat an animal. If one of them were
gifted she might find poetic expression for that meaning.

The sharp distinction between the moral and the psychological,
and the tendency to think that expressions of moral impossibility
are really misleading ways of expressing a sense of obligation, are
aspects of what I have called meaning-neglect. But the interdepen-
dencies between modalities of possibility and necessity, and coming
to see the meaning of something, go beyond what is naturally called
morality. M said that she couldn't just have more children in the way
she thought Vietnamese women could. Her sense that it was impossible for her was inseparable from her sense of what it means to have
a child and from her sense of what distinguishes her and her kind

essentially from the Vietnamese. Nonetheless, the impossibility she expressed is not a moral impossibility. Nor, I think, is the impossibility that I would have shot a rabbit that day on the hill, or the impossibility that Orwell would have shot the fascist soldier holding up his trousers. Like the impossibility that we should consign our dead to the rubbish collection or that we should routinely number rather than name our children, they are impossibilities that structure and are structured by that part of the realm of meaning in which morality is embedded.

In Coetzee's *The Lives of Animals*, Elizabeth Costello imagines a world in which we fully understand the suffering and the indignity we inflict on animals. At the end she appears to be at the edge of madness, but one doesn't know whether this is the cause or the effect of her sense of the evils to which we are all accomplices.

It is both, I think. She compares the slaughter of animals and our indifference to it to the Holocaust and to people's indifference to it when it happened:

> I return one last time to the places of death all around us, the places of slaughter to which, in a huge communal effort, we close our hearts. Each day a fresh holocaust, yet, as far as I can see, our moral being is untouched. We do not feel tainted. We can do anything, it seems, and come away clean.
>
> We point to the Germans and Poles and Ukrainians who did and did not know of the atrocities around them. We like to think they were inwardly marked by the after-effects of

that special form of ignorance. We like to think that in their nightmares the ones whose suffering they had refused to enter came back to haunt them. We like to think they woke up haggard in the mornings and died of gnawing cancers. But probably it was not so. The evidence points in the opposite direction: that we can do anything and get way with it; that there is no punishment.

At the end of the book she says to her son with tears in her eyes:

It's that I no longer know where I am. I seem to move around perfectly easily among people, to have perfectly normal relations with them. Is it possible, I ask myself, that all of them are participants in a crime of stupefying proportions? Am I fantasizing it all? I must be mad! Yet every day I see the evidences. The very people I suspect produce the evidence, exhibit it, offer it to me. Corpses. Fragments of corpses that they have bought for money.

It is as if I were to visit friends, and to make some polite remark about the lamp in their living room, and they were to say, 'Yes, it's nice, isn't it? Polish-Jewish skin it's made of, we find that's best, the skins of young Polish-Jewish virgins.' And then I go to the bathroom and the soap-wrapper says, 'Treblinka—100% human stearate.' Am I dreaming, I say to myself? What kind of house is this?

Yet I'm not dreaming. I look into your eyes, into Norma's, into the children's, and I see only kindness, human-kindness. Calm down, I tell myself, you are making a mountain out of a molehill. This is life. Everyone else comes to terms with it, why can't you? *Why can't you?*

The reasons why the Allies fought against Germany were complex, but many people believe rightly that the Holocaust itself would have proved sufficient reason. But, as I have already said, no one responds, and I think no one can seriously wish to respond, to the slaughter of animals as though it justified taking up arms against farmers, butchers and people who work in abattoirs. That can hardly be irrelevant to how we should understand the moral character of our indifference to the slaughter of animals. It must also inform the moral character of any other analogies we may be tempted to draw between the Holocaust and our treatment of animals. People have said that the Holocaust and the way we now kill animals are examples of 'the industrialisation of death', as though the radical differences between Auschwitz and a modern abattoir do not deprive the comparison of power to shed light.

Can I say that after quoting such a forceful passage? The force of the passage is in its rhetoric rather than in its moral clarity. Or, at any rate, when I step back to assess critically its undeniable power, I find nothing in it that would make me revise my claim that I cannot, and that I know no one else who can, respond to the killing of animals as though it were mass murder. The analogy Costello draws is, I believe, foolish and also offensive, but not because of anything distinctive to the Holocaust. People have argued that the Holocaust is unique and mysterious. On that, I offer no comment here. But the comparison between Auschwitz and an abattoir is not offensive because of anything that might distinguish Auschwitz from a camp in the Gulag or from any other occurrence of mass murder. It is offensive because we do not and cannot respond to what happens in the abattoir as we respond to murder. To invoke the particular evil of the Holocaust as a reason to be offended by what Costello says is as misguided and, I suspect, as offensive as what she says.

One need not be susceptible to such extravagant comparisons in order fully to acknowledge that our cruelty to animals is abominable and to hope that future generations will find it so. One hopes that they will be incredulous that we could be so cruel, and that practices that are now current and unexceptionable will then be crimes. Provided that one keeps clearly and firmly in mind the qualifications that follow from my criticism of Costello's comparison of our practices with the Holocaust, then there need be nothing absurd in her fear that we will be judged to have been 'participants in a crime of stupefying proportions'. Does that mean that people like my father were morally deficient in their relationship to animals because they killed them for food?

During the worst of the drought of the 1980s my father had thirty or so goats. He had them because he felt sorry for a goat with a broken leg he had seen at the market. He bought it only so that he could tend to its injury but, when the goat's leg mended, my father thought it should have company and so he bought it a mate. From those two he eventually got thirty and they brought him nothing but hard work and sorrow.

The period of the drought was heartbreaking for anyone on a farm. Cattle and sheep were slaughtered in their thousands and buried in mass graves because there was no feed for them. The price of meat had fallen so low that a semi-trailer load of animals would not pay the truck driver's fee. When my father ran out of feed for his goats he cut grass at the side of the road with a scythe, trailer after trailer load, month after month. At the time he was over sixty years old and the work placed great strain on his health. The farmers in the region who saw him at work and saw its results—grass cut for fifteen or so kilometres along the road from Maryborough to Castlemaine—were astonished that he would work so hard and risk his health for animals, especially since they knew that he earned nothing from them. One of those farmers said to me, 'I can work hard. I know it. But nothing like that.' One day, cutting grass, my father collapsed with pain in his chest and left arm.

Occasionally my father killed a goat to eat, but mostly he killed them to feed to his dogs. He had very little money with which to buy meat, for he and his wife lived off their pensions, a good portion of which went to pay vets' fees for their animals. When my daughter Eva heard that he sometimes killed his goats she was distressed. Fond of animals, she enjoyed visiting my father because there were almost always baby chickens, or ducklings or calves or kids to be seen. Sometimes one of them would be living in the kitchen, sick and in need of warmth. 'How could he do it?' she asked me. Really she meant how could he, of all people, he who cares so much. I asked her if she knew anyone or had even heard of anyone who was kinder to animals than her grandfather. 'No,' she said.

I did not mean to suggest to Eva that our conversation should settle questions she had about whether it was right to kill animals for food. I did hope, though, that she would learn something about what it might mean to kill them. She wanted to know how her grandfather could care so much for animals yet kill them, kill the very animals, indeed, for whom he worked so hard and for whom he risked his health. Her first response was to think that the fact that he killed animals showed that he cared less for them than she had thought. My question to her made her realise that his preparedness to kill animals need show no defect in his compassion for them.

Instinctively Eva knew that she could not just say that if my father killed animals then, by definition, he must be lacking in true compassion for them. How, after all, does one learn about compassion, about how deep it can go and what its limits are, if not by reflection on authoritative examples of it? It was, I suspect, because my father was so at one with the natural world, so pitying of it because of the hurt human beings have inflicted on it, that his example had such authority for Eva. But for his example to be rightly authoritative his compassion would have to be clear-sighted about what it means to kill an animal.

There are wonderful people, people whose compassion for animals is as deep as my father's was, who find it morally impossible to kill an animal, and whose finding it so is interdependent with their understanding of what it means to kill an animal for food. Their example, however, does not, for me, show up my father. No one I have known has been more appreciative than he was of the generosity with which animals give themselves to us and grateful for the grace they bring to our lives. We sometimes find something morally impossible for us, but do not think that people who find it possible are thereby mistaken, let alone morally deficient. Even examples of great and pure authority can rightly speak differently to people. On this matter, therefore, I can only speak personally.